Sadlier

WE•BELIEVE™

God Loves Us

WITH PROJECT DISCIPLE

Pray
Learn
Celebrate
Share
Choose
Live

Grade One

Sadlier

This advanced publication copy has been printed prior to final publication and pending ecclesiastical approval.

Acknowledgments

Excerpts from the English translation of *The Roman Missal*, © 2010, International Committee on English in the Liturgy, Inc. All rights reserved.

Excerpts from the English translation of the *Catechism of the Catholic Church* for the United States of America, copyright © 1994, United States Catholic Conference, Inc.—Libreria Editrice Vaticana. English translation of the *Catechism of the Catholic Church: Modifications from the Editio Typica* copyright © 1997, United States Catholic Conference, Inc.—Libreria Editrice Vaticana. Used with permission.

Scripture excerpts are taken from the *New American Bible* with *Revised New Testament and Psalms* Copyright © 1991, 1986, 1970, Confraternity of Christian Doctrine, Inc., Washington, D.C. Used with permission. All rights reserved. No part of the *New American Bible* may be reproduced by any means without permission in writing from the copyright owner.

Excerpts from the English translation of *Rite of Baptism of Children* © 2017, International Committee on English in the Liturgy, Inc. (ICEL); excerpts from the English translation of *Lectionary for Mass* © 1969, 1981, 1997, ICEL; excerpts from the English translation of *Rite of Penance* © 1974, ICEL; excerpts from the English translation of *A Book of Prayers* © 1982, ICEL; excerpts from the English translation of *The Liturgy of the Hours* © 1974, ICEL; excerpts from the English translation of *Book of Blessings* © 1988, ICEL. All rights reserved.

Excerpts from *Catholic Household Blessings and Prayers (Revised Edition)* copyright © 2007, 1988 United States Catholic Conference Inc. Washington, D.C. Used with permission. All rights reserved.

English translation of the Glory to the Father, Lord's Prayer, Nicene Creed, and Apostles' Creed by the International Consultation on English Texts. (ICET)

Excerpt from the homily of Pope Francis, Solemnity of All Saints, November 1, 2013, and from his *Evangelii Gaudium, Apostolic Exhortation on the Proclamation of the Gospel in Today's World*, November 24, 2013, copyright © Vatican Publishing House, Libreria Editrice Vaticana.

Gaudium et Spes, Pastoral Constitution of the Church in the Modern World, Pope Paul VI, December 7, 1965.

Excerpt from Saint Augustine of Hippo, *The Literal Interpretation of Genesis*, Book X, Chapter 23, Verse 39, from The Church Fathers, http://www.churchfathers.org/

Excerpt from the encyclical *Pacem in terris (Peace on Earth)*, by Pope John XXIII, April 11, 1963, copyright © Libreria Editrice Vaticana.

"We Believe, We Believe in God," © 1979, North American Liturgy Resources (NALR), 5536 NE Hassalo, Portland, OR 97213. All rights reserved. Used with permission. "People Worry," © 1993, Daughters of Charity and Christopher Walker. Published by OCP Publications, 5536 NE Hassalo, Portland, OR 97213. All rights reserved. Used with permission. "Children of God," Michael B. Lynch. Copyright © 1977, Raven Music. All rights reserved. Used with permission. "Jesus Wants to Help Us," music and text © 1999, Christopher Walker and Paule Freeburg, DC. Published by OCP Publications, 5536 NE Hassalo,

Portland, OR 97213. All rights reserved. Used with permission. "In the House of Our God," © 1988, 1989, 1990, Christopher Walker. Published by OCP Publications, 5536 NE Hassalo, Portland, OR 97213. All rights reserved. Used with permission. "Sing for Joy," © 1999, Bernadette Farrell. Published by OCP Publications, 5536 NE Hassalo, Portland, OR 97213. All rights reserved. Used with permission. "Share the Light," © 1999, Bernadette Farrell. Published by OCP Publications, 5536 NE Hassalo, Portland, OR 97213. All rights reserved. Used with permission. "We Are the Church," © 1991, Christopher Walker. Published by OCP Publications, 5536 NE Hassalo, Portland, OR 97213 All rights reserved. Used with permission. "We Are the Church" was originally from "Come, Follow Me" Music Program, Benziger Publishing Company. "Advent Song," Words/Music by MaryLu Walker © 1975, 1998, 16 Brown Road, Corning, New York 14830. All rights reserved. Used with permission. "Open Our Hearts," © 1989, Christopher Walker. Published by OCP Publications, 5536 NE Hassalo, Portland, OR 97213. All rights reserved. Used with permission. "We Celebrate with Joy," © 2000, Carey Landry. Published by OCP Publications, 5536 NE Hassalo, Portland, OR 97213. All rights reserved. Used with permission. "Celebrate God," © 1973, North American Liturgy Resources (NALR), 5536 NE Hassalo, Portland, OR 97213. All rights reserved. Used with permission. "Walk in the Light," © 1996, Carey Landry. Published by OCP Publications, 5536 NE Hassalo, Portland, OR 97213. All rights reserved. Used with permission. "Children of God," © 1991, Christopher Walker. Published by OCP Publications, 5536 NE Hassalo, Portland, OR 97213. All rights reserved. Used with permission. "Awake, Arise and Rejoice!" © 1992, Marie-Jo Thum. Published by OCP Publications, 5536 NE Hassalo, Portland, OR 97213. All rights reserved. Used with permission. "Shout From the Mountains," © 1992, Marie-Jo Thum. Published by OCP Publications, 5536 NE Hassalo, Portland, OR 97213. All rights reserved. Used with permission. "We Come to Share God's Special Gift," © 1991, Christopher Walker. Published by OCP Publications, 5536 NE Hassalo, Portland, OR 97213. All rights reserved. Used with permission. "Walk in Love," © 1990, North American Liturgy Resources (NALR), 5536 NE Hassalo, Portland, OR 97213. All rights reserved. Used with permission. "Joseph Was a Good Man," music and text © 1999, Christopher Walker and Paule Freeburg, DC. Published by OCP Publications, 5536 NE Hassalo, Portland, OR 97213. All rights reserved. Used with permission. "Malo, Malo, Thanks Be to God," © 1993, Jesse Manibusan. Administered by OCP Publications, 5536 NE Hassalo, Portland, OR 97213. All rights reserved. Used with permission. "Alleluia No. 1," Donald Fishel. © 1973, WORD OF GOD MUSIC (Administered by THE COPYRIGHT COMPANY, Nashville, TN). All rights reserved. International copyright secured. Used with permission. "Jesus Wants to Help Us," music and text © 1999, Christopher Walker and Paule Freeburg, DC. Published by OCP Publications, 5536 NE Hassalo, Portland, OR 97213. All rights reserved. Used with permission.

Printed in the United States of America

S® is a registered trademark of William H. Sadlier, Inc.

WeBelieve™ is a trademark of William H. Sadlier, Inc.

William H. Sadlier, Inc.
25 Broadway
New York, NY 10004-1010

ISBN: 978-0-8215-3051-1

9 10 11 12 13 WEBC 25 24 23 22 21

The Subcommittee on the Catechism, United States Conference of Catholic Bishops, has found the doctrinal content of this series, copyright 2015, to be in conformity with the *Catechism of the Catholic Church*.

The Sadlier *We Believe* Program was drawn from the wisdom of the community. It was developed by nationally recognized experts in catechesis, curriculum, and child development. These teachers of the faith and practitioners helped us to frame every lesson to be age-appropriate and appealing. In addition, a team including respected catechetical, liturgical, pastoral, and theological experts shared their insights and inspired the development of the program.

Contributors to the inspiration and development are:

Dr. Gerard F. Baumbach
Professor Emeritus, Institute for Church Life
Director Emeritus of the Echo Program
University of Notre Dame

Carole M. Eipers, D.Min.
Vice President, Executive Director
    of Catechetics
William H. Sadlier, Inc.

Theological Consultants

His Eminence Donald Cardinal Wuerl, M.A., S.T.D.
Archbishop of Washington

Most Reverend Edward K. Braxton, Ph.D., S.T.D.
Official Theological Consultant
Bishop of Belleville

Reverend Joseph A. Komonchak, Ph.D.
Professor Emeritus of Theology and Religious Studies
The Catholic University of America

Most Reverend Richard J. Malone, Th.D.
Bishop of Buffalo

Reverend Monsignor John E. Pollard, S.T.L.
Pastor, Queen of All Saints Basilica
Chicago, IL

Scriptural Consultant

Reverend Donald Senior, CP, Ph.D., S.T.D.
Member, Pontifical Biblical Commission
President Emeritus of Catholic Theological Union
Chicago, IL

Catechetical and Liturgical Consultants

Patricia Andrews
Director of Religious Education
Our Lady of Lourdes Church,
Slidell, LA

Reverend Monsignor John F. Barry, P.A.
Pastor, American Martyrs Parish
Manhattan Beach, CA

Reverend Monsignor John M. Unger
Deputy Superintendent for Catechesis
    and Evangelization
Archdiocese of St. Louis

Thomas S. Quinlan
Director, Religious Education Office
Diocese of Joliet

Curriculum and Child Development Consultants

Brother Robert R. Bimonte, FSC
President, NCEA

Sr. Carol Cimino, SSJ, Ed.D.
Superintendent, Catholic Schools
Diocese of Buffalo

Gini Shimabukuro, Ed.D.
Professor Emeritus
Catholic Educational Leadership Program
School of Education
University of San Francisco

Catholic Social Teaching Consultants

John Carr
Director
Initiative on Catholic Social Thought and Public Life
Georgetown University

Joan Rosenhauer
Executive Vice President, U.S. Operations
Catholic Relief Services
Baltimore, MD

Inculturation Consultants

Allan Figueroa Deck, S.J., Ph.D., S.T.D.
Rector of Jesuit Community
Charles Casassa Chair of Catholic Social Values
Professor
Loyola Marymount University

Kirk P. Gaddy, Ed.D.
Middle School Team Leader/Religion Teacher
St. Francis International School
Silver Spring, MD

Reverend Nguyễn Việt Hưng
Vietnamese Catechetical Committee

Dulce M. Jiménez-Abreu
Director of Bilingual Programs
William H. Sadlier, Inc.

Mariology Consultant

Sister M. Jean Frisk, ISSM, S.T.L.
International Marian Research Institute
Dayton, OH

Media/Technology Consultants

Sister Judith Dieterle, SSL
Past President, National Association of
    Catechetical Media Professionals

Robert Methven
Vice President, Digital Publisher
William H. Sadlier, Inc.

Robert T. Carson
Media Design Director
William H. Sadlier, Inc.

Writing/Development Team

Rosemary K. Calicchio
Executive Vice President, Publisher

Blake Bergen
Director of Publications

Joanne McDonald
Editorial Director

Regina Kelly
Supervising Editor

William M. Ippolito
Director of Corporate Planning

Martin Smith
Planning and Analysis
    Project Director

Dignory Reina
Editor

Peggy O'Neill
Digital Content Manager

Contributing Writers
Susan Anderson
Christian Garcia
Kathy Hendricks
Shannon Jones
Theresa MacDonald
Gloria Shahin

Suzan Laroquette
Director of Catechetical
    Consultant Services

Judith A. Devine
National Sales Consultant

Victor Valenzuela
National Religion Consultant

Publishing Operations Team

Carole Uettwiller
Vice President of Planning and
    Technology

Vince Gallo
Senior Creative Director

Francesca O'Malley
Art/Design Director

Cheryl Golding
Production Director

Monica Reece
Senior Production Manager

Jovito Pagkalinawan
Electronic Prepress Director

Design/Image Staff
Kevin Butler, Nancy Figueiredo,
Stephen Flanagan, Lorraine Forte,
Debrah Kaiser, Cesar Llacuna,
Bob Schatz, Karen Tully

Production Staff
Monica Bernier, Robin D'Amato,
Rachel Jacobs, Carol Lin,
Vincent McDonough,
Yolanda Miley, Laura Rotondi,
Allison Stearns

We are grateful to our loyal *We Believe* users whose insights and suggestions have inspired *We Believe: Catholic Identity Edition*—the premier faith formation tool built on the six tasks of catechesis.

Contents

UNIT 2

We Are Followers of Jesus 93

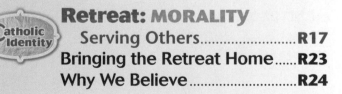

UNIT 4

We Celebrate and Live Our Faith

The *We Believe* program will help us to

learn

celebrate

share

and live our Catholic faith.

Throughout the year we will hear about many saints and holy people.

Saint Andrew Kim Taegon

Saint Anne

Saint Francis of Assisi

Saint Francis Xavier

Saint John Vianney

Saint Joseph

Saint Katharine Drexel

Saint Patrick

Saints Peter and Paul

Pope Pius X

Saint Teresa of Avila

Blessed Teresa of Calcutta

Together, let us grow as a community of faith.

Welcome!

✝ We Gather in Prayer

Leader: Welcome everyone to Grade 1 *We Believe*.

As we begin each chapter, we gather in prayer. We pray to God together.

Let us sing the *We Believe* song!

♫ We Believe in God

We believe in God;

We believe, we believe in Jesus;

We believe in the Spirit who gives us life.

We believe, we believe in God.

11

Each day we learn more about God.

WE GATHER

We begin by taking a moment to pray.

✝ *Thank you, God, for our classmates.*

Then we

think about

talk about

write about

draw about

act out

Life

at home

in our neighborhood

at school

in our parish

in our world

Talk about your life right now.

WE BELIEVE

We learn about

- God the Father, God the Son, and God the Holy Spirit
- Jesus, the Son of God, who became one of us
- the Church and its teachings.

We find out about the different ways Catholics live their faith and celebrate God's love.

is an open Bible. When we see it with a blue Scripture reference, what follows is a paraphrase of the Bible. When we see a black reference like this (John 13:34), that passage is directly from the Bible.

Each of these signs points out something special that we are going to do.

means that we will make the Sign of the Cross and pray as we begin our lesson.

Key Words means it is time to review the important words we have learned in the day's lesson.

means we have an activity. We might

talk   write   act   sing

draw   work together   imagine

There are all kinds of activities!

As Catholics...

Here we discover something special about our faith. Don't forget to read it!

means it's time to sing! We sing songs we know, make up our own songs, and sing along with those in our *We Believe* music program.

WE RESPOND

We can respond by

- thinking about ways our faith affects the things we say and do
- sharing our thoughts and feelings
- praying to God.

Then in our homes, neighborhood, school, parish, and world, we can say and do the things that show love for God and others.

When we see **We Respond** we think about and act on what we have learned about God and our Catholic faith.

In this space, draw yourself as a *We Believe* first grader.

We are so happy you are with us!

Show What you Know

We "show what we know" about each chapter's content. A disciple is always learning more about his or her faith.

We sharpen our disciple skills with each chapter's Project Disciple pages!

Picture This Pictures are a way for us to see and show our disciple skills.

Grade 1 Chapter 9

PROJECT

Show What you Know

Match the sentence parts.

The Temple •

Easter Sunday •

• is the special day we celebrate that Jesus Christ rose to new life.

• was the holy place in Jerusalem where the Jewish People prayed.

Celebrate!

Circle the ways you can celebrate that Jesus died and rose for us.

Pray

Praise

Sing

116 www.webelie...

DISCIPLE

Picture This What does this stained glass window show?

Jesus is our _____

_____

Reality Check

The Church teaches us to respect all workers. People work in our neighborhood to protect and care for us. Who helps to protect and care for you?

☐ Police officers

☐ Firefighters

☐ People who keep my neighborhood clean

☐ People in my parish and school

Take Home

What are the two words of praise you learned in this chapter?

_____

_____

Say these words as a family.

117

Celebrate!

As disciples, we worship God.

Reality Check

Here we get to "check-off" our ideas and choices.

Take Home

We always get the chance to share our faith "at home."

There are **LOADS of ACTIVITIES** that make us better disciples! Just look at this additional list.

What's the Word?—all about Scripture

Question Corner—take a quiz

Fast Facts—learn even more about our faith

Make It Happen—living out what we have learned

What Would You Do?—making the right choices

Pray Today—talking and listening to God

Saint Stories—finding great role models

More to Explore—getting information from the Internet and library

Now, Pass It On!—invites us to witness to our faith

Don't forget to look for the **Disciple Challenge**—count how many you can do this year!

And every chapter ends with a Chapter Test!

We Believe
Catholic Identity Edition

You are on a journey to continue to grow as a disciple of Jesus Christ. You can strengthen your Catholic Identity through these new features:

Catholic Identity Retreats

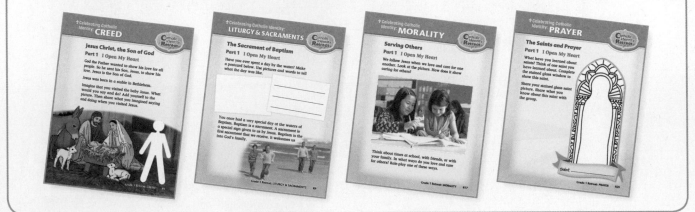

Bringing the Retreat Home

Why We Believe As a Catholic Family

Catholic Identity Q & A

Catholic Identity Home Companion

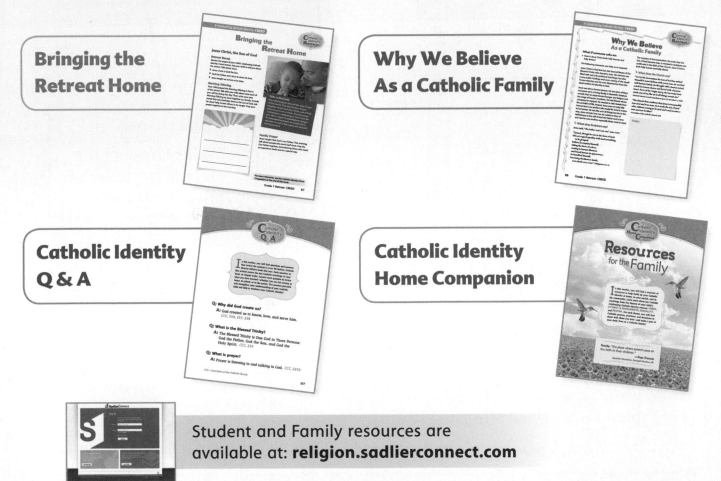

Student and Family resources are available at: **religion.sadlierconnect.com**

Jesus Christ, the Son of God

Part 1 I Open My Heart

God the Father wanted to show his love for all people. So he sent his Son, Jesus, to show his love. Jesus is the Son of God.

Jesus was born in a stable in Bethlehem.

Imagine that you visited the baby Jesus. What would you say and do? Add yourself to the picture. Then share what you imagined saying and doing when you visited Jesus.

Jesus Christ, the Son of God

Part 2 We Come Together for Prayer

Leader: Repeat after me as we pray:
Jesus, you are the Son of God. We love you.

All: Jesus, you are the Son of God. We love you.

Leader: Jesus, you are our Lord. We honor you.

All: Jesus, you are our Lord. We honor you.

Leader: Jesus, you show us God the Father's love.
We praise you.

All: Jesus, you show us God the Father's love.
We praise you.

Leader: Sign your name to the note to Jesus.

Jesus, I love you.

Greyson

Jesus is the Son of God the Father. Jesus taught that God is our Father, too. Let us love God as Jesus taught us.

All: Amen.

Jesus Christ, the Son of God

Part 3   I Cherish God's Word

"From the cloud came a voice that said, 'This is my beloved Son . . . listen to him.'" (Matthew 17:5)

LISTEN to the reading from Scripture. Pay close attention to the reading.

REFLECT on what you heard. Think about:

- What God said.

- How can you listen to Jesus?

SHARE your thoughts and feelings with God in prayer. Speak to God as a friend.

CONTEMPLATE or sit quietly and think about God's Word in the Scripture passage from the Gospel of Matthew above.

Jesus Christ, the Son of God

Part 4   I Value My Catholic Faith

When we pray, we can use our own words. We can also pray without words. We can sit quietly and think about how close we are to Jesus.

We honor Jesus when we pray. We can pray:
Jesus Christ, Son of God, be with us.

(Based on the Jesus Prayer)

Make a prayer card for this Jesus Prayer. Trace the words. Draw a picture of Jesus or a symbol that makes you think of him. Remember Jesus loves you.

Share your prayer cards.

Jesus Christ, Son of God, be with us.

Jesus Christ, the Son of God

Part 5 I Celebrate Catholic Identity

Jesus Christ, God the Son, showed us God the Father's love. Jesus used words to show us God's love. He used actions to show us God's love. We follow Jesus when we love God, love ourselves, and love others.

Together think of an action that answers each question. Take turns acting out the answers.

How do we show that we love God?
How do we show that we love ourselves?
How do we show that we love others?

Jesus Christ, the Son of God

Part 6 I Honor My Catholic Identity

(*All pray the Sign of the Cross.*)

Leader: Jesus shows us how to love. We want to follow Jesus in all we say and do. Listen to God's Word.

"Whatever you do, in word or in deed, do everything in the name of the Lord Jesus, giving thanks to God the Father through him."
(Colossians 3:17)

Let us pray a special prayer. It is called the "Morning Offering." As we pray, think of one thing you can do or say today to follow Jesus.

All: My God, I offer you today
all that I think and do and say,
uniting it with what was done
on earth, by Jesus Christ,
your Son. Amen.

Catholic Identity Retreat

Bringing the Retreat Home

Jesus Christ, the Son of God

Retreat Recap

Review the pages of your child's *Celebrating Catholic Identity: Creed* retreat. Ask your child to tell you about the retreat. Talk about Jesus:

- Jesus Christ is God the Son.
- God the Father sent Jesus to show his love.
- Jesus taught us to love as he does.

Morning Offering

Your child prayed the Morning Offering in Part 6 of the retreat. Talk with your child about what each of you will be doing this day. Then write your own Morning Offering to Jesus together as a family. Include words that acknowledge Jesus as the Son of God. Ask for Jesus' help to love others as he taught. Pray your prayer together in the morning.

Take a Moment

Your child prayed a form of the Jesus Prayer in the retreat. Pray the full Jesus Prayer together aloud: *Lord Jesus Christ, Son of God, have mercy on me, a sinner.* Pray the prayer several times, meditating on Jesus' love for you. This is a type of contemplative prayer. In contemplative prayer, we simply allow ourselves to rest in the experience of God's loving presence.

Family Prayer

Jesus taught that God is our Father. This evening, talk about people who need God's love. Pray the Our Father together, remembering those who need to experience God's love in a special way.

For more resources, see the *Catholic Identity Home Companion* at the end of this book.

Why We Believe
As a Catholic Family

What if someone asks us:

- How is Jesus Christ both fully human and fully divine?

The following resources can help us to respond:

Jesus Christ is God the Son, the Second Person of the Blessed Trinity who became man. His ministry was filled with not only profound teachings, but also many public healings and even raising of the dead! These miracles and his own Resurrection from the dead confirm his identity as God.

Jesus was also a human person. He was born of Mary and grew up in a loving family in Nazareth. Scripture reveals that he experienced hunger and fatigue and the range of human emotions. He had friends whose company he enjoyed. He needed to take breaks from the activities of life. Indeed, Jesus was not only fully human but is our perfect role model for what it means to be human. He was like us in all things but sin. In this way, Jesus reveals how we are called to lives of faithfulness to the will of God the Father and to love and care for one another, especially those most in need.

❧ What does Scripture say?

Jesus said, "The Father and I are one" (John 10:30).

"[Jesus], though he was in the form of God,
did not regard equality with God something
   to be grasped.
Rather, he emptied himself,
taking the form of a slave,
coming in human likeness;
and found human in appearance,
he humbled himself,
becoming obedient to death,
   even death on a cross." (Philippians 2:6–8)

The mystery of the Incarnation, the truth that the Son of God became man, is revealed in Scripture and confirmed in the faith of the Church. Jesus Christ is both fully human and fully divine.

❧ What does the Church say?

"For by His incarnation the Son of God has united Himself in some fashion with every man. He worked with human hands, He thought with a human mind, acted by human choice and loved with a human heart. Born of the Virgin Mary, He has truly been made one of us, like us in all things except sin."
(Second Vatican Council, *Gaudium et Spes*, 22, December 7, 1965)

"The Church thus confesses that Jesus is inseparably true God and true man. He is truly the Son of God who, without ceasing to be God and Lord, became a man and our brother."
(*Catechism of the Catholic Church*, 469)

Notes:

Jesus Teaches Us About God's Love

Seasonal Chapters

PROJECT DISCIPLE
DEAR FAMILY

Pray Learn Celebrate Share Choose Live

In Unit 1 your child will grow as a disciple of Jesus by:

- learning about God the Father's love for all people
- praying to the Blessed Trinity: God the Father, God the Son, and God the Holy Spirit
- meeting Jesus, the Son of God, and the Holy Family
- understanding what Jesus taught us about loving God, ourselves, and others
- living the Great Commandment that Jesus taught.

What Would *you* do?

God wants us to care for all creation. As a family, decide on one way you can do each of the following:

Save water _____

Recycle _____

Add to the beauty of creation _____

Care for animals _____

Pray Today This week, make the Sign of the Cross your special family prayer. You may also want to bless each other at bedtime by tracing a cross on each other's forehead.

Reality Check

"Education in the faith by the parents should begin in the child's earliest years." *(Catechism of the Catholic Church, 2226)*

Picture This

Together look at the artwork on pages 48, 49, and 51 of the text. Talk about the Holy Family. What are Jesus, Mary, and Joseph doing in the pictures? How did they help each other and show their love for each other? Then talk about the ways your family members help and show love to one another.

What's *the* Word?

Read the Gospel passage from Luke on page 60 in the text. Talk together about the ways God shows he cares for your family. Ask each member to share one way he or she knows God cares. Then offer a prayer of thanks for God's love!

Take Home

Each chapter in your child's *We Believe* Grade 1 text offers a "Take Home" activity that invites your family to support your child's journey to more fully become a disciple of Christ.

Be ready for this unit's Take Home:

Chapter 1: Appreciating God's gifts in the world

Chapter 2: Praying as a family

Chapter 3: Making a family activity collage

Chapter 4: Helping people who are sick

Chapter 5: Learning about people of different cultures

God Is Our Father

✝ We Gather in Prayer

Let us show our thanks to God
by singing this song.

🎵 **Thank You, God** *("London Bridge")*

Thank you, God, for Earth, our home,
Earth, our home, Earth, our home.
Thank you, God, for Earth our home.
We say, "Thank you."

Use the same tune to sing about
these gifts in God's world.

- Thank you, God, for birds and fish.
- Thank you, God, for bugs that crawl.
- Thank you, God, for vegetables.
- Thank you, God, for everything.

God created the world.

✝ *Thank you, God, for our world.*

Look at the picture.
Which things are your favorite?
Tell why.

WE BELIEVE

The word *create* means "to make."
God made everything.
God created our wonderful world.
Creation is everything God made.

📖 Genesis 1:1–31

Read Along

God created light and water. God created fruits and vegetables. God created all kinds of animals.

God created people. Then "God looked at everything he had made, and he found it very good." (Genesis 1:31)

20

We read about God's creation
in the Bible.
The Bible is a special book
about God.
The **Bible** is the book of God's Word.

We believe that God is our Father.
We believe that everything he
created is good.

WE RESPOND

God created our
wonderful world.
What makes the world
so wonderful for you?

creation everything
God made

Bible the book of
God's Word

 Draw something beautiful
you saw today.

Now pray together.
God, thank you for everything
you made. God, you are wonderful.

God created all people.

✝ *God, thank you for the gift of creation.*

Name some of your family members. What makes each one special to you?

WE BELIEVE

God wanted to share his love.
So he created people.
We were created to know, love, and serve God.

We are God's special creation.
God did not create everyone to be exactly alike.
Every person is special to God.

God wants people to take care
of his gift of creation.
He wants us to take care
of his world.

How are the people in the pictures
taking care of God's world?

WE RESPOND

What are some ways you can
take care of God's world?

Draw a picture to finish
this prayer.

God, I take care of your world when I

God gives us special gifts.

✝ *God our Father, we love you.*

What do plants and animals
do each day?
What do we do?

We can do many things that animals
and plants cannot do.

We can:

- think and learn.

- care for God's world.

- share love with our families
  and friends.

- listen to and talk to God.

These things are gifts from God.
God gives us these gifts so we can
know and love him.

People can help us to do these things.
People are gifts from God, too.
People help us to grow in God's love.

WE RESPOND

Who are the people who help you to grow in God's love?

Write the first letters of their names on the flower.
Thank God for these helpers.

As Catholics...

We believe that God created angels. Angels are God's helpers. But they do not have bodies like people do. Angels give people messages from God. They protect and guide us. They never stop praising God.

How can you praise God, too?

God promises to love us always.

WE GATHER

✝ *God, we want to grow in your love forever.*

What does the word *forever* mean?

⚡ Find another word for *forever*. Color the letters in the flowers.

A L W A Y S

WE BELIEVE

God our Father loves us very much. He wants us to love him. In the Bible, there is a story about Adam and Eve.

📖 Genesis 2—3

Read Along

Adam and Eve lived in the most beautiful garden in the world. Everything was perfect there. God gave them everything they needed to live.

God wanted them to be happy with him forever.

One day Adam and Eve did something God had told them not to do. Then they had to live in a world that was not perfect any more.

God never stopped loving Adam and Eve.
He promised that he would be with them always.
He promised to send someone to help them and their children.

God our Father promises to be with us and love us always, too.
He promises again and again to save all people.

WE RESPOND

It is important for us
to remember God's promises.
What did God promise?

Put your right hand over
your heart.
Pray these words or use
your own words.
Thank you, God, for loving me always.
I promise to love you in return.

27

PROJECT

Show What you Know

Match the **Key Words** to the pictures.

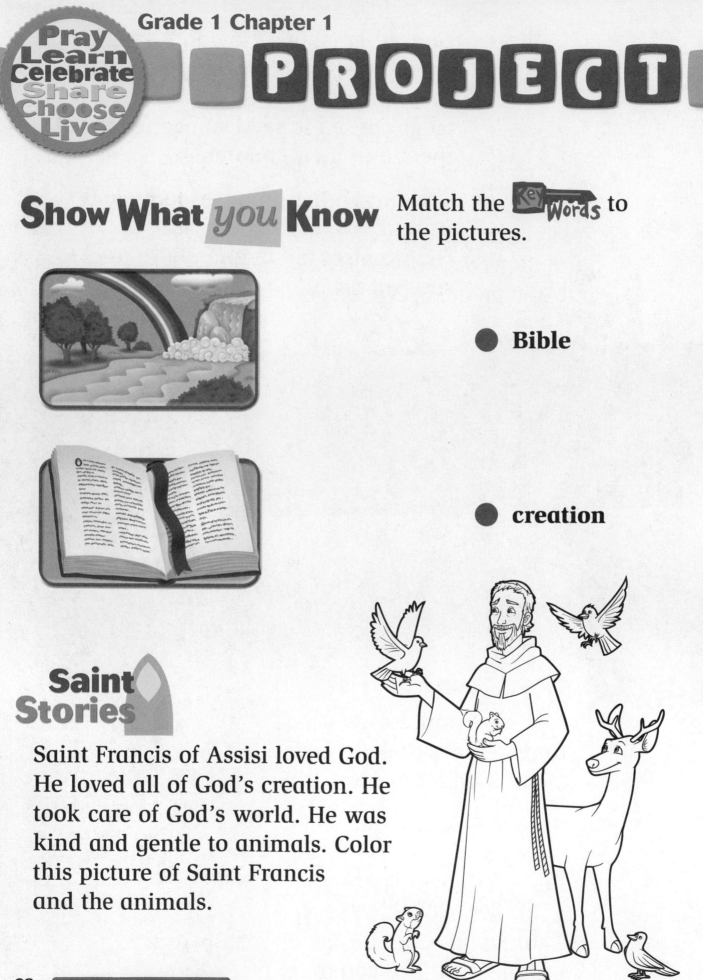

● **Bible**

● **creation**

Saint Stories

Saint Francis of Assisi loved God. He loved all of God's creation. He took care of God's world. He was kind and gentle to animals. Color this picture of Saint Francis and the animals.

DISCIPLE

Pray
Learn
Celebrate
Share
Choose
Live

Make *it* Happen

Think about God's gifts of people, plants, and animals. Which of these are you most thankful that God created? Circle your choices.

People

Plants

Animals

Reality Check

Check ways you can take care of God's world.

❏ Recycle

❏ Love my family

❏ Try not to be wasteful

❏ Take care of myself

Take Home

Take a walk with your family. Talk about the things you see that God made.

Together say a prayer to thank God for his creation.

CHAPTER TEST

Circle the correct answer.

1. All things made by God are _____.

   little   good

2. God created all _____ to know and love him.

   people   animals

3. The Bible is a special _____ about God.

   book   picture

4. God _____ create everyone to be exactly alike.

   did   did not

5. God promises to love us _____.

   only at special times   always

 How can people care for all God's creation?

We Believe in the Blessed Trinity

✝ We Gather in Prayer

Let us stand to celebrate God's love.
For each action pray together,
"We thank you, God.
We celebrate your love."

Prayer Actions

- Raise your arms in the air.

- Clap your hands.

- Put your hands over your hearts.

- Close your eyes and bow your heads.

God sent his own Son, Jesus, to us.

WE GATHER

✝ *God, we celebrate your love for us.*

Have you ever waited for something
good to happen?
How did you feel while you
were waiting?

WE BELIEVE

People waited for God to keep
his promise to help us.
God the Father had a plan
for keeping his promise.
At a special time he sent his
own Son to us.

God sent Jesus to live with us
on earth.
God sent an angel to ask Mary
to be the Mother of his own Son, Jesus.
Jesus showed us

- how much God loves us

- how to love God

- how to love ourselves

- how to love one another.

Jesus promised to help us, too!
He promised to send the Holy Spirit.
Jesus promised that the Holy Spirit
would always be our Helper.

WE RESPOND

Read each message. Color in the face
that shows how each message makes you feel.

- God loves you very much.

- God sent Jesus to us.

- Some people do keep promises.

- Some people do not keep promises.

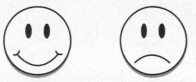

What messages make you feel happy?

Pray:

God our Father, you kept your promise.
You sent your Son to help us.
Help us to keep the promises we make.

Jesus is God's greatest gift.

WE GATHER

✝ *God, thank you for sending Jesus to us.*

Name one gift you would like to receive on your birthday.

WE BELIEVE

God's greatest gift to us is Jesus.
Jesus is the Son of God who became one of us.
Jesus is our brother and our friend.

Jesus tells us about God's love.
He tells us that God is our loving Father.

Jesus said, "As the Father loves me, so I also love you." (John 15:9)

We always have the gift of Jesus' love. Here is a story about his special love.

Read Along

"And people were bringing children to him. . . but the disciples rebuked them. When Jesus saw this he became indignant and said to them, 'Let the children come to me.'"
(Mark 10:13, 14)

WE RESPOND

🧍 Why is Jesus God's greatest gift? Add yourself to the picture.

There are Three Persons in One God.

WE GATHER

✝ *Jesus, thank you for showing us God's love.*

Join hands to make a circle. Where is the end of the circle? How can a circle remind us about God's love?

WE BELIEVE

Jesus, the Son of God, taught us about God the Father and God the Holy Spirit.

The **Blessed Trinity** is One God in Three Persons.

- God the Father is the First Person of the Blessed Trinity.
- God the Son is the Second Person of the Blessed Trinity.
- God the Holy Spirit is the Third Person of the Blessed Trinity.

God the Father, God the Son, and God the Holy Spirit are joined in love.

Jesus taught that we should be united in love as the Blessed Trinity is. Our love for one another resembles the unity of the Blessed Trinity.

Key Word

Blessed Trinity One God in Three Persons: God the Father, God the Son, and God the Holy Spirit

WE RESPOND

Sometimes pictures can help us to understand what we believe about the Blessed Trinity.

Look at the picture of the three circles joined together. Use one crayon to color the circles.

What can this picture help you to remember about the Blessed Trinity?

Pray:

God the Father, God the Son,
God the Holy Spirit,
we believe you are joined in love.

As Catholics...

We honor Saint Patrick. Saint Patrick went to Ireland to teach the people about God. He showed them a shamrock to help them learn about the Blessed Trinity. A shamrock is a plant that has three leaves. It can remind us about the Three Persons in One God. Pray to the Blessed Trinity often.

The Sign of the Cross is a prayer to the Blessed Trinity.

WE GATHER

✝ *God the Father, God the Son, and God the Holy Spirit, we praise you.*

What are these children doing? What do you think they are thinking or saying?

WE BELIEVE

When we pray, we show our love for God.
Prayer is listening to and talking to God.

Sometimes when we pray, we use special words from the Bible.
Sometimes we use our own words.
Sometimes we say prayers written by other people.

For some prayers we use actions as we pray.
The **Sign of the Cross** is a prayer to the Blessed Trinity:

In the name of the Father,
and of the Son,
and of the Holy Spirit.
Amen.

We begin our prayers by praying these words.

1. In the name of the Father,

2. and of the Son,

3. and of the Holy

4. Spirit.

5. Amen.

WE RESPOND

Let us stand now and pray the Sign of the Cross.

The Sign of the Cross always reminds us that we believe in the Blessed Trinity.

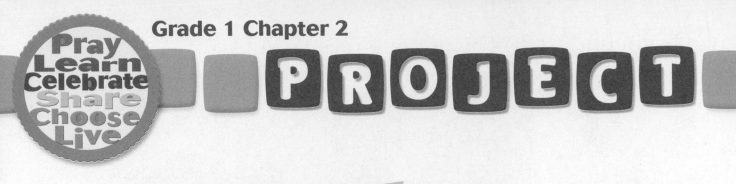

PROJECT

Show What *you* Know

Trace the Key Words. Talk about each one.

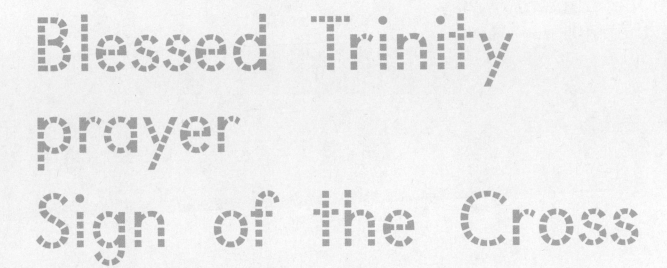

Blessed Trinity

prayer

Sign of the Cross

Picture This

Who is God's
greatest gift?
Draw him here.

Pray
Learn
Celebrate
Share
Choose
Live

Celebrate!

Draw a line to match the pictures to the words. Then, pray the Sign of the Cross.

> In the name of the Father,

> Amen.

> and of the Holy

> Spirit.

> and of the Son,

Fast Facts

Catholics begin the Mass by making the Sign of the Cross. This shows they believe in the Blessed Trinity.

Take Home

Prayer is listening to and talking to God. You can pray as a family. Together, say this prayer.

Thank you, God, for the gift of your Son, Jesus.

Circle the correct answer.

1. Is the Holy Spirit our Helper?

    Yes   **No**

2. Is prayer only talking to God?

    Yes   **No**

3. Did God keep his promise by sending his own Son, Jesus, to us?

    Yes   **No**

4. Is there only one God?

    Yes   **No**

5. Are we praying only to God the Father when we pray the Sign of the Cross?

    Yes   **No**

 Who are the Three Persons of the Blessed Trinity?

Jesus Grew Up in a Family

✝ We Gather in Prayer

Leader: Let us stand and pray together. For our families, that we may all keep growing in God's love, we pray,

All: God, please help us to share your love.

Leader: For families who are going to welcome new babies soon, we pray,

All: God, please help them to grow in your love.

Leader: For families who do not have everything they need to live, we pray,

All: God, please help us to take care of them.

God chose Mary to be the Mother of his Son.

WE GATHER

✝ *God, we need your love and your care.*

🏃 Look at each picture.
If it shows people today, circle NOW.
If it shows people in the time of Jesus, circle THEN.

NOW

THEN

NOW

THEN

44

WE BELIEVE

God loved Mary very much.
Mary always did what God wanted.

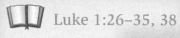 Luke 1:26–35, 38

Read Along

One day God sent an angel to a young girl named Mary. The angel told her not to be afraid. The angel told her that she was going to have a son. Mary was also told to name the child Jesus.

The angel said to Mary, "Therefore the child to be born will be called holy, the Son of God." (Luke 1:35)

Mary told the angel that she would do what God wanted.

Mary is the Mother of God's only Son, Jesus.
Jesus loves his mother.
He wants us to love her, too.

WE RESPOND

Mary did what God asked of her.
We can, too.
What is one thing God asks you to do today?

Ask Mary for help. Pray together:
Holy Mary, Mother of God, pray for us.

45

Jesus was born in Bethlehem.

WE GATHER

✝ *God our Father, thank you for Jesus, your Son.*

Where do you live?
Have you lived in other places?

WE BELIEVE

Mary married a man named Joseph.
They lived in the town of Nazareth.
Mary was going to have a baby.
Mary and Joseph were waiting
for Jesus to be born.

Read Along

"In those days a decree went out from Caesar Augustus that the whole world should be enrolled. . . . So all went to be enrolled, each to his own town. And Joseph too went up from Galilee . . . to the city of David that is called Bethlehem . . . to be enrolled with Mary, his betrothed, who was with child. While they were there, the time came for her to have her child, and she gave birth to her firstborn son. She wrapped him in swaddling clothes and laid him in a manger, because there was no room for them in the inn." (Luke 2:1, 3–7)

God the Father loved us so much. He sent his Son into the world. At **Christmas** we celebrate the birth of Jesus.

One way we celebrate is by sharing the story of what happened when Jesus was born.

WE RESPOND

What would you tell your family and friends about the birth of Jesus?

Christmas the time when we celebrate the birth of Jesus

As Catholics...

Each year during the nine days before Christmas, Catholics in Mexico and other countries act out the story of Mary and Joseph on their way to Bethlehem. People take part in this outdoor play called *Las Posadas*. In English these words mean "The Inns." The actors who play Mary and Joseph go from house to house. But no one will let them in until the last day. Then the person playing the innkeeper lets them in. Then the rest of the people enter and celebrate the birth of Jesus.

How do you celebrate the birth of Jesus?

Jesus lived in Nazareth with Mary and Joseph.

WE GATHER

✝ *Jesus, you are in our hearts always.*

Talk about ways your family helps you to do your best in school.
Talk about ways you help your family when someone is not feeling well.

WE BELIEVE

We call Jesus, Mary, and Joseph the **Holy Family**.
The Holy Family lived in Nazareth.
Uncles and aunts and cousins lived there, too.
Jesus and his family loved and cared for one another.

Jesus obeyed Mary and Joseph.
He did what Mary and Joseph asked him to do.

Holy Family the family of Jesus, Mary, and Joseph

WE RESPOND

Think about ways Jesus, Mary, and Joseph helped one another. What are ways you will help your family?

Read the following sentences. Color the heart only if it is next to a way you can help your family.

♡ Take turns choosing TV programs.

♡ Make fun of people.

♡ Play fair.

♡ Obey my parents or those who care for me.

♡ Be mean to my brothers, sisters, or friends.

Pray quietly.

Jesus, help me to be like you. I want to help my family, too.

The Holy Family obeyed God the Father and prayed to him.

WE GATHER

✝ *Jesus, Mary, and Joseph, please help our families to love God.*

Imagine that the Holy Family is coming to visit. Draw a picture to show your family getting ready.

WE BELIEVE

Jesus, Mary, and Joseph believed
in the one, true God.
They loved God very much.
They obeyed God's laws.
They helped each other at home.
They helped other people.
They obeyed the laws of their country.

The Holy Family prayed to God.
They prayed every morning and
every night.
They joined other Jewish families
for prayer each week.
They listened to stories about
God and his people.

WE RESPOND

When does your family pray together?
Share this prayer at your family meals.

Bless us, O Lord,
and these your gifts
which we are about to
receive from your goodness.
Through Christ our Lord.
Amen.

Pray
Learn
Celebrate
Share
Choose
Live

PROJECT

Show What you Know

Christmas

Holy Family

Write the Key Words into the word shapes.

Then, talk about each one.

Picture This

Fill in this picture story.

God sent an angel to Mary.

Jesus was born in Bethlehem.

The Holy Family lived in Nazareth.

DISCIPLE

Pray
Learn
Celebrate
Share
Choose
Live

Celebrate!

Complete the chart. Use words or pictures.

What are some ways you celebrate your birthday?	What are some ways you celebrate Jesus' birth?

Reality Check

Check your favorite ways to help your family.

❑ Clean my room

❑ Listen

❑ Be kind

❑ Pray for my family members

❑ _____

(your own way)

Take Home

Gather some family magazines. Find pictures of families doing things together. Make a collage of the different things that *your* family members do together. Talk about ways your family is like the Holy Family.

53

CHAPTER TEST

Circle the correct answer.

1. Jesus was born in _____.

Bethlehem   Nazareth

2. When Jesus was growing up, the Holy Family lived in _____.

Bethlehem   Nazareth

3. We celebrate the birth of Jesus on _____.

Christmas   Easter

4. Mary _____ did what God asked her to do.

always   never

5. Jesus, Mary, and _____ were members of the Holy Family.

the angel   Joseph

TALK ABOUT IT What are some of the things the Holy Family did together?

Jesus Works Among the People

✝ We Gather in Prayer

♫ Jesus in the Morning

Jesus, Jesus,
Jesus in the morning,
Jesus at the noontime;
Jesus, Jesus,
Jesus when the sun goes down!

Love him, love him,
Love him in the morning,
Love him at the noontime;
Love him, love him,
Love him when the sun goes down!

John the Baptist helped people to get ready for Jesus.

WE GATHER

✝ *Jesus, be with us always.*

Have you ever helped get ready to welcome a special visitor at home?
At school?
What did you do to help?

WE BELIEVE

John was the cousin of Jesus.
When John grew up, he went to live in the desert.
He became one of God's helpers.

God gave John an important message to share.
John told people to put God first in their lives.
John told them not to be selfish.
He told them to share and be fair.

Many people heard John's message.
John, called John the Baptist, was
getting the people ready.
They were getting ready to welcome
Jesus, the Son of God, into their lives.
Jesus would show them the way God
wanted them to live.

WE RESPOND

You need to be ready to
welcome Jesus every day.

Circle one way you can
welcome Jesus.

Share with my friends.

Say my prayers.

Be fair when I play.

Say "please" and "thank you."

Help my family at home.

What other ways can you
welcome Jesus?

Jesus shared God's love with all people.

✝ *Jesus, welcome into our lives.*

Think about the people you see in your town.
What are they like? What do they do?

When Jesus was a grown-up, he left his home in Nazareth.
He went from town to town teaching people.
He told them about God and his great love.

Jesus treated all people with respect.
He shared the news of God's love with everyone. He shared with

- children and parents
- farmers and fishermen
- poor people and rich people
- those who were sick and those who were healthy.

58

Here is a story about someone Jesus met.

📖 Luke 19:1–5

Read Along

One day Jesus visited a town called Jericho. A large crowd gathered to see Jesus. A very rich man named Zacchaeus wanted to see Jesus, too. Zacchaeus was so short that he could not see above the heads of the other people. He climbed a tree and sat in the branches so that he could see Jesus.

When Jesus came to the tree, he looked up. He said, "Zacchaeus, come down quickly, for today I must stay at your house." (Luke 19:5)

Zacchaeus was very happy. Jesus was coming to his house. Jesus knew that Zacchaeus needed to hear the news of God's love, too.

WE RESPOND

🧍 Act out the story of Zacchaeus. What did you learn about Jesus from this story?

Thank Jesus for sharing God's great love.

Jesus teaches that God watches over us and cares for us.

WE GATHER

✝ *God, we need your love always.*

What are some things that are important to you?
Show how you take care of one of them.

WE BELIEVE

Jesus wanted people to know about God.
He wanted everyone to know that
God takes care of them.

 Luke 12:22–24

Read Along

One day Jesus was teaching. He pointed to the birds flying above the crowd. Jesus said that the birds did not have to worry about food. God cares for the birds. Jesus told the crowd that God cares for people even more! He said, "How much more important are you than birds!" (Luke 12:24)

Do you know how important we are to God?
God watches over us all the time.
He loves and takes care of us even when we do not know it.
When we believe someone loves us, we **trust** them.
Jesus tells us to trust God.

WE RESPOND

How does God watch over you?

trust to believe in someone's love for us

♫ People Worry

People worry about this and that.
People worry about this and that!
But Jesus tells us, "Don't worry.
Don't worry about this and that!"

God knows ev'rything we need,
    just believe, just believe.
God takes care of ev'ryone.
Trust in God, trust in God.

As Catholics...

We all need to take quiet time to pray to God. We can praise God. We can thank God. We can ask God for help. Before Jesus began to teach, he went into the desert. He went there to pray to God.

Where is your special place to pray?

Jesus helped all those in need.

WE GATHER

✝ *Jesus, thank you for teaching that God cares for us.*

How do you know that someone loves and cares for you?
What does the person say?
What does the person do?

WE BELIEVE

Jesus cared for all people.
He welcomed and blessed the children.
He comforted people who were sad
or afraid.

Jesus helped the poor.
He fed the hungry.
He healed many people who were sick.
He loved everyone, even those who did
not like him.

Read Along

"A great crowd followed [Jesus]. Two blind men were sitting by the roadside, and when they heard that Jesus was passing by, they cried out, '[Lord,] Son of David, have pity on us!'. . . Jesus stopped and called them and said, 'What do you want me to do for you?' They answered him, 'Lord, let our eyes be opened.' Moved with pity, Jesus touched their eyes. Immediately they received their sight, and followed him." (Matthew 20:29–30, 32–34)

WE RESPOND

What do you think the two men said after Jesus healed them?

Finish this prayer. Match each picture to the right words.

Jesus,

- Open my ___s. May they *see* people who need help.

- Help my ___s to *hear* your word.

- Let my ___s *do* good for others.

PROJECT

Show What you Know

Write a sentence using the Key Word trust.

_____

- -

_____

What Would you do?

Jess spilled her snack during snack time. She felt sad and hungry. Henry wanted to help Jess.

In the ⬯ write what Henry could say to Jess.

Pray
Learn
Celebrate
Share
Choose
Live

Make *it* Happen

Jesus shared the news of God's love with everyone. Draw one way you can share the news of God's love.

Pray Today

Praying for people is another way to help and love them. Think of someone you know who needs your love. Say a prayer for this person.

↳ **DISCIPLE CHALLENGE** Pray your prayer with friends and family.

Take Home

Circle one way your family can share God's love with people who are sick:

• praying for or with them

• cheering them up

• listening to them

• reading Bible stories to them.

• _____
(another way)

CHAPTER TEST

Circle the correct answer.

1. Was Zacchaeus the cousin of Jesus?

Yes   No

2. When we trust God, do we believe in his love for us?

Yes   No

3. Did Jesus treat all people with respect?

Yes   No

4. Did Jesus show God's love by healing the sick?

Yes   No

5. Did Jesus stay in Nazareth all his life on earth?

Yes   No

 What did John the Baptist tell people?

Jesus Teaches Us About Love

✝ We Gather in Prayer

Leader: • Jesus, you blessed the children who came to see you. We ask you to bless us now.

All: • Jesus, bless our eyes so we may see your love.

• Jesus, bless our ears so we may hear your words of love.

• Jesus, bless our hands so we may share your love.

• Jesus, bless our mouths so we may tell others about your love.

• Jesus, fill our hearts with love.

Many people wanted to follow Jesus.

WE GATHER

✝ *Jesus, bless us.*

Think about the people you know.
Who do you like to spend time with?
Why?

WE BELIEVE

Jesus traveled from place to place.
News about him spread everywhere.
Many people went looking for Jesus.

When Jesus taught, crowds of people
would come to hear him.
One day Jesus even had to get on a boat
so all the people could see and hear him.

Why did crowds of people come to Jesus?
The people needed him to:

- make them feel better

- teach them to pray

- tell them the Good News
  about God's love

- tell them how to live a better life.

After spending time with Jesus, people came to know what God's love was like.
Jesus made everyone feel special.

WE RESPOND

How can you spend time with Jesus?

Circle each thing you can do.

- Pray.

- Listen to a story about Jesus.

- Share Jesus' love with others.

69

Jesus taught the Great Commandment.

WE GATHER

✝ *Jesus, we want to follow you.*

What is one of your family's rules?
How does keeping this rule help you and
your family?

WE BELIEVE

Commandments are laws or rules given
to us by God. These laws help us to live as
God wants us to.

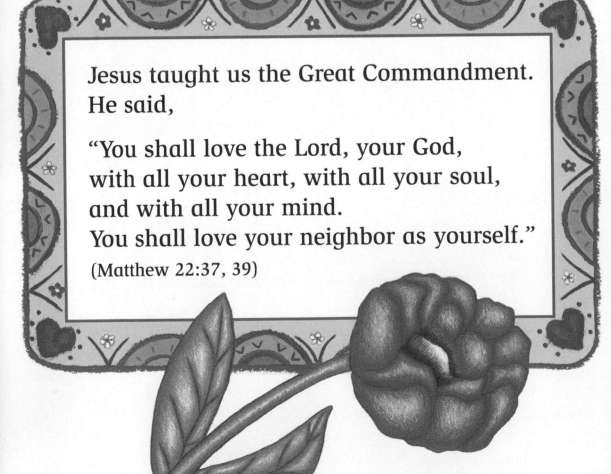

Jesus taught us the Great Commandment.
He said,

"You shall love the Lord, your God,
with all your heart, with all your soul,
and with all your mind.
You shall love your neighbor as yourself."

(Matthew 22:37, 39)

When we follow this commandment,
we do what God wants us to do.
We love God, ourselves, and others.

We show God our love in these ways.

- We do what God wants us to do.
- We go to Mass on Sunday.
- We pray to God everyday.
- We make the Sign of the Cross with respect.

commandments
laws or rules given to us by God

WE RESPOND

What are other
ways you can
show your love for God?

Pray these words.
My God, I offer you today all
I think and do and say.

As Catholics...

When we wake up in the morning, we can pray to God. This shows how important God is to us. There are special prayers we say to offer God our whole day. We call these prayers morning offerings. You can say the prayer on this page as a morning offering.

Jesus taught us to love God, ourselves, and others.

WE GATHER

✝ *God the Father, God the Son, and God the Holy Spirit, help us.*

You show love for yourself when you eat the right foods.
What other things can you do to show that you love yourself?

WE BELIEVE

When we learn about Jesus' teaching, we learn about love.
God made us to show us his love.
We show God we love ourselves when we take care of ourselves.
We can share our love with others, too.

SOAP

Jesus showed us how to love people.
He was kind.
He listened to people's problems.
He cared for all people.
Jesus wants us to act as he acted.
We do this when we love God, ourselves,
and others.

WE RESPOND

Say a prayer to Jesus. Ask Jesus to help
you to love others as he did.

Look at the pictures. Color the
star beside the pictures that show
people acting as Jesus did.

Jesus taught us that all people are our neighbors.

WE GATHER

✝ *Jesus, help us to love others as you did.*

Who are your neighbors? How do you help them?

WE BELIEVE

After Jesus taught the Great Commandment, someone asked who our neighbors are. Jesus answered by telling this story.

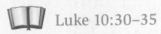 Luke 10:30–35

Read Along

One day a man was walking down the road. Robbers hurt him and took his money. They left the man on the side of the road.

A priest walked by the person who was hurt. He did not stop to help. Then another religious leader passed and saw the hurt man. But he kept walking. Finally, a man from the country called Samaria stopped to help him. He rubbed oil on the man's cuts and covered them with bandages. The Samaritan brought the hurt man to a roadside inn.

The next day the Samaritan had to leave. He said to the innkeeper, "Take care of him. If you spend more than I have given you, I shall repay you on my way back." (Luke 10:35)

Which man was a good neighbor?
The good neighbor was the man
from Samaria.
We call him the good Samaritan.
He cared for and helped the hurt man.

Jesus told this story to help us
understand that:

- all people are our neighbors
- we are to be good neighbors to
  everyone.

WE RESPOND

How can you be a good neighbor in
your school or neighborhood this week?

Stand and shake hands with those who
are near you.

♫ Good Neighbors
(*"Go 'Round and 'Round the Village"*)

Let's try to be good neighbors!
Let's try to be good neighbors!
Let's try to be good neighbors
   as Jesus wants us to.

PROJECT

Show What *you* Know

What are the laws or rules given to us by God?

_____

- -

_____

What Would *you* do?

Follow the path that will bring you closer to Jesus. Use the sign posts to help you.

START

Cheat

Respect

Love

FINISH

Pray

Help

Fight

Listen

SCHOOL

Share

Tease

Hurt

Break

Lie

DISCIPLE

Pray Learn Celebrate Share Choose Live

Make *it* Happen

Be a good neighbor. Circle one item from each column and do it today.

Who will you help?	What will you do?
A classmate	Be kind
A family member	Share a story about Jesus
Someone you know in your parish	Teach him or her a prayer

↳ **DISCIPLE CHALLENGE** How are the family members in the picture showing their love for God and one another?

Take Home

Jesus taught us that we are all neighbors. We can show love for our neighbors. With your family, learn more about your neighbors who are from or living in other countries.

CHAPTER TEST

Circle the correct answer.

1. Jesus taught us that _____ people are our neighbors.

   all   some

2. _____ people came to hear Jesus.

   Many   Few

3. We show God our love when we _____.

   hurt others   love ourselves

4. Commandments are _____ given to us by God.

   laws   tests

5. Jesus _____ people's problems.

   forgot about   listened to

What did Jesus teach us in the story of the good Samaritan?

Praise to you, Lord Jesus Christ.

SEASONAL

CHAPTER 6

This chapter presents an overview of the Church Year.

The Church praises Jesus all year long.

WE GATHER

What does the word *praise* mean to you?

WE BELIEVE

All year long the Church gathers to thank God for his great love. Together, we praise God. We celebrate all that Jesus did for us.

Every year we have special times to praise and thank God. Each year we join together to celebrate these special times.

Read Along

Advent is a time of waiting. We wait and get ready for the coming of the Son of God.

Christmas is a time to celebrate the birth of the Son of God. We celebrate God's greatest gift to us, his Son, Jesus.

Lent is a time to remember all that Jesus has done for us. We get ready for the Church's great celebration.

The Three Days are the Church's greatest celebration. We remember and celebrate that Jesus died for us and rose to new life.

Easter is a time of great joy. We rejoice and celebrate that Jesus rose to new life.

Ordinary Time is when we celebrate everything about Jesus, especially his life and teachings.

Advent

Christmas

Ordinary Time

Lent

Three Days

Easter

Ordinary Time

The Church year helps us to follow Jesus. The different times help us remember and celebrate all that Jesus did for us. The times also help us remember that Jesus is with us today!

All during the year we thank Jesus for the gift of himself. We thank him for being with us always.

WE RESPOND

 In the empty space, draw something or someone for whom you are thankful to Jesus.

✝ We Respond in Prayer

Leader: During the Church year we celebrate that Jesus is with us all the time.

Leader: We pray in Advent:

All: Come, Lord Jesus!

Leader: We pray during Christmas:

All: Rejoice! Jesus is born!

Leader: We pray in Lent:

All: Lord, have mercy.

Leader: We pray during the Three Days:

All: Jesus, bring us new life.

Leader: We pray during Easter:

All: Alleluia! Christ is risen!

Leader: We pray in Ordinary Time:

All: Praised be the name of Jesus!

Leader: We remember that Jesus is with us each and every day of the year.

All: Praised be the name of Jesus!

Pray Learn Celebrate Share Choose Live

PROJECT DISCIPLE

Celebrate!

Read and guess this riddle about a special time of the Church year.

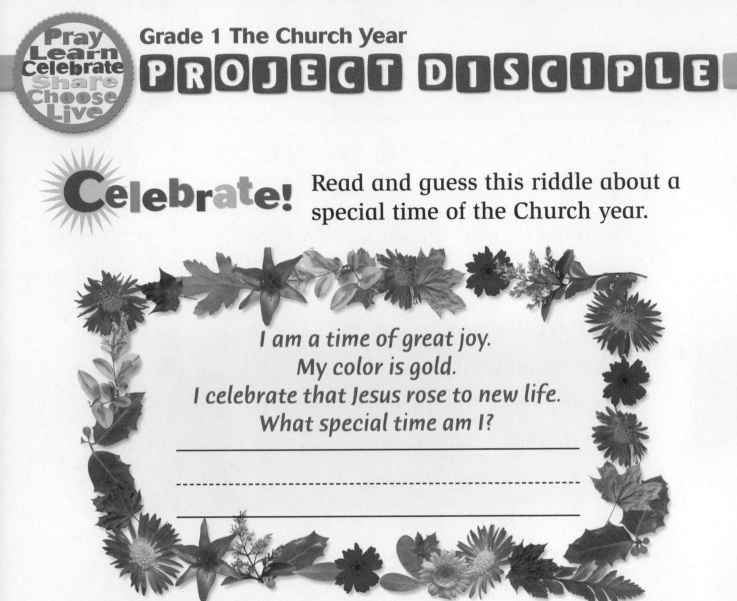

I am a time of great joy.
My color is gold.
I celebrate that Jesus rose to new life.
What special time am I?

_____

- -

_____

Now, write your own riddle about a different special time of the Church year. Ask a classmate to guess the answer.

_____

- -

_____

_____

- -

_____

Take Home

See if your family members can guess the riddle you have written. Ask them to write one too!

↳ **DISCIPLE CHALLENGE** With your family, write riddles for each special time of the Church year.

Give thanks to the Lord,
his love is everlasting.

SEASONAL

CHAPTER 7

This chapter helps us to understand
the season of Ordinary Time.

The Church celebrates the life and teachings of Jesus.

WE GATHER

We can put things in order by numbering them.

What is the biggest number of things that you have put in order?

WE BELIEVE

The Church has special times to celebrate. During Ordinary Time, we celebrate the life and teachings of Jesus. We try to follow him more closely each day. This season is called Ordinary Time because the Church puts the Sundays in number *order*.

Every Sunday of the year is a special day. Every Sunday we celebrate the Mass. We remember the things Jesus has done for us. We thank Jesus for the gift of himself.

We hear wonderful stories about

- Jesus' teaching, healing, and forgiving
- the first followers of Jesus
- the Holy Spirit helping the first members of the Church.

Look at the pictures on these pages. Which one shows Jesus teaching? Which one shows him healing? Which one tells us something about the first followers of Jesus?

Share your answers.

Saints are followers of Jesus who loved him very much. The saints have died, but they now live forever with God. The lives of the saints show us how to be followers of Jesus.

We celebrate many special days during Ordinary Time. One of them is called All Saints' Day. It is celebrated on November 1.

WE RESPOND

Draw yourself here. Write one way you are a follower of Jesus.

✠ We Respond in Prayer

Leader: We are all children of God. On All Saints' Day, we celebrate all the children of God who are living forever with God. They are called saints.

Reader: Let us listen to the Word of God.

"Blessed are the peacemakers,
    for they will be called children
        of God." (Matthew 5:9)

The Gospel of the Lord.

All: Praise to you, Lord Jesus Christ.

Leader: The saints are children of God. We honor them because they loved God and loved others. We are children of God. We can love God and love others, too!

♫ Children of God

Children of God is what we are.
Children of God we all must be.
Children of God; that's you and me.
Thanks be to God.
Thanks be to God.
We all stand in need to be thankful
    for making us children of God.

PROJECT DISCIPLE

Celebrate!

Trace this special message! Decorate the banner.

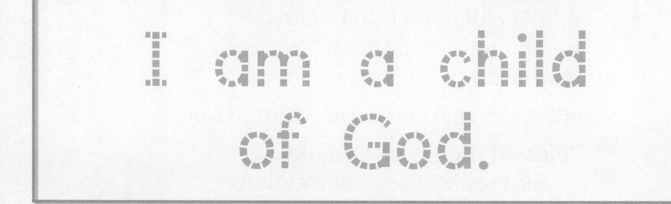

I am a child of God.

What's the Word?

Jesus said, "Love one another as I love you" (John 15:12).

Check the ways Jesus showed his love.

- ❏ Teaching
- ❏ Healing
- ❏ Forgiving
- ❏ Helping

Take Home

As a family, talk about ways you follow Jesus everyday. Write them below.

Everyday, we follow Jesus by

_____

_____

UNIT TEST

Fill in the circle beside the correct answer.

1. The Bible is a special book about _____.

○ God ○ trees

2. God sent his own Son, _____, to us.

○ Joseph ○ Jesus

3. On Christmas, we celebrate the birth of _____.

○ Jesus ○ Joseph

4. Jesus taught us that we should be good neighbors to _____.

○ everyone ○ people we know

Circle the correct answer.

5. Was Jesus mean to people? **Yes** **No**

6. Did God create the world? **Yes** **No**

7. Did Jesus teach us that God watches over us and cares for us? **Yes** **No**

8. Was Zacchaeus Jesus' only follower? **Yes** **No**

continued on next page **91**

Look at the two pictures below.
For each picture, write what Jesus is doing
and saying.

9.

_____

- - - - - - - - - - - - - - - - - -

_____

- - - - - - - - - - - - - - - - - -

_____

_____

- - - - - - - - - - - - - - - - - -

_____

10.

_____

- - - - - - - - - - - - - - - - - -

_____

_____

- - - - - - - - - - - - - - - - - -

_____

- - - - - - - - - - - - - - - - - -

_____

We Are Followers of Jesus

Seasonal Chapters

DEAR FAMILY

In Unit 2 your child will grow as a disciple of Jesus by:

- appreciating that Jesus had many followers, and he taught them to pray
- understanding that Jesus died and rose to bring us new life
- learning that Jesus Christ sent the Holy Spirit to his followers
- hearing the story of Pentecost, and the ways the Holy Spirit helps the Church to grow
- recognizing that the pope and bishops lead the Church in caring for and serving others.

Celebrate!

This image is a model of the Temple in Jerusalem during Jesus' time. Jesus was Jewish, and so the roots of our Catholic faith are Jewish. If you have Jewish friends, invite them for a meal and celebrate your common heritage. Pray for all Jewish People.

Show That You Care

In Chapter 12 your child will learn about the pope and the bishops. Help your child to name the Church leaders. (Visit your parish Web site.)

Our pope is _____

Our bishop is _____

Our pastor is _____

Our parish ministers are _____

Together thank God for those who serve the Church today.

94

Reality Check

"Parents' respect and affection are expressed by the care and attention they devote to bringing up their young children and *providing for their physical and spiritual needs*."

(*Catechism of the Catholic Church*, 2228)

Pray Today

Pray the Lord's Prayer together. Talk about the ways your family can help the Kingdom of God to grow. Remind your child that you always pray the Lord's Prayer at Mass on Sunday.

Fast Facts

The Church uses several symbols to represent the Holy Spirit: a flame, a dove, clouds and light, a hand, and others. In your church, look for any symbols for the Holy Spirit. Which symbol means the most to your family?

Take Home

Each chapter in your child's *We Believe* Grade 1 text offers a "Take Home" activity that invites your family to support your child's journey to more fully become a disciple of Christ.

Be ready for this unit's Take Home:

Chapter 8: Praying the Lord's Prayer together

Chapter 9: Praising God

Chapter 10: Joining the parish for breakfast

Chapter 11: Making a Holy Spirit poster

Chapter 12: Pledging to serve others

Jesus Had Many Followers

✝ We Gather in Prayer

♪ Jesus Wants to Help Us

We believe Jesus wants to help us.
We believe Jesus wants to help us.
We believe that Jesus
    always wants to help us.

When we pray, Jesus wants to hear us.
When we pray, Jesus wants to hear us.
We believe that Jesus
    always wants to hear us.

Jesus invited people to be his followers.

WE GATHER

✝ *Jesus, please help us to be your followers.*

🏃 Act out how you feel when you get a special invitation from a friend.

WE BELIEVE

Jesus invited people to come and be with him.
He asked people to be his followers.
Here is a story about our friend Jesus and his first followers.

Read Along

"As [Jesus] was walking by the Sea of Galilee, he saw two brothers, Simon who is called Peter, and his brother Andrew, casting a net into the sea; they were fishermen. He said to them, 'Come after me, and I will make you fishers of men.' At once they left their nets and followed him." (Matthew 4:18–20)

Jesus asked other men and women to be his followers, too. Those who became his followers learned from him.

They tried to act as Jesus did. They shared God's love with others as Jesus did. They became his friends.

Jesus had many followers. The **Apostles** were the twelve men Jesus chose to lead his followers.

Jesus invites each of us to be his follower, too.

If you want to be a follower of Jesus, write your name here.

_____

_____

WE RESPOND

Why do you want to be a follower of Jesus?

How can you follow him?

Jesus' followers believed that he was the Son of God.

WE GATHER

✝ *Jesus, we believe that you are the Son of God.*

When are some times you need help? Who helps you?

WE BELIEVE

Jesus spent a lot of time with his followers.
They trusted Jesus very much.
Here is a story about a time when Jesus helped his followers.

📖 Luke 8:22–25

Read Along

One day Jesus was in a boat with his followers. He fell asleep. Soon a storm started rocking the boat. Jesus' followers were afraid. They woke Jesus up. They believed he would help them.

Jesus told the winds and waves to be still. Jesus' followers were amazed because the storm stopped. They asked, "Who then is this, who commands even the winds and the sea, and they obey him?" (Luke 8:25)

🏃 Act out the story.

Jesus did amazing things to
help people.
Jesus calmed the storm.
He did many things that only God
can do.
Jesus' followers saw these things and
believed in him.
They believed Jesus was the Son of God.

WE RESPOND

Imagine that you were on that boat
with Jesus.
What would you have said to Jesus
after he calmed the storm?

What will you do to show that you
believe in Jesus?

Pray together.
Jesus, Son of God, we believe in you.

Jesus showed his followers how to pray.

WE GATHER

✝ *Jesus, you are always with us.*

Talk about something you have learned by listening to others.

Talk about something you have learned by watching other people.

WE BELIEVE

Jesus often prayed to God the Father. Sometimes Jesus prayed alone. Sometimes he prayed with other people.

Jesus' followers learned to pray by watching him pray.
They learned to pray by listening to Jesus, too.

 Luke 11:1–2

Read Along

One day Jesus was praying. When he was finished, one of his followers asked him to teach the group to pray.

Jesus told his followers, "When you pray, say: 'Father, hallowed be your name.'" (Luke 11:2)

We call the prayer Jesus taught his followers the **Lord's Prayer**.
We also call this prayer the Our Father.
Here are the words we pray.

Our Father, who art in heaven,
hallowed be thy name;
thy kingdom come;
thy will be done on earth as it is in
    heaven.
Give us this day our daily bread;
and forgive us our trespasses
as we forgive those who trespass
    against us;
and lead us not into temptation,
but deliver us from evil.
Amen.

Decorate the prayer frame.

As Catholics...

Lord is another name for God. Jesus' followers sometimes called him Lord. We use the name *Lord* in many of our prayers. When we do this, we remember that Jesus is the Son of God.

During Sunday Mass, listen for the times we pray, "Lord."

WE RESPOND

Who teaches you to pray?
Why do you pray?

We pray the Lord's Prayer.

WE GATHER

✝ *Jesus, teach us to pray as you did.*

 Draw a picture to show a time you prayed with your family.

WE BELIEVE

Jesus taught his followers the Lord's Prayer.

We can pray this prayer with others or by ourselves.

The Lord's Prayer	When we pray this prayer:
Our Father, who art in heaven,	We praise God. We pray to God as our loving Father.
hallowed be thy name;	We say that God is holy. We honor and respect his name.
thy kingdom come; thy will be done on earth as it is in heaven.	We ask that all people will know and share God's love. This is what God wants for all of us.
Give us this day our daily bread;	We ask God to give us what we need. We remember all people who are hungry or poor.
and forgive us our trespasses as we forgive those who trespass against us;	We ask God to forgive us. We need to forgive others.
and lead us not into temptation, but deliver us from evil. Amen.	We ask God to keep us free from anything that goes against his love.

Make up actions for the Lord's Prayer.

WE RESPOND

When do you hear the Lord's Prayer prayed?
Gather in a circle. Pray the Lord's Prayer together.

PROJECT

Pray
Learn
Celebrate
Share
Choose
Live

Show What you Know

Apostles

Lord's Prayer

Write the Key Word that answers each question.

What is the prayer Jesus taught his followers?

_____

- -

_____

Who are the twelve men Jesus chose to lead his followers?

_____

- -

_____

✛ Pray Today

Many fishermen in France pray this prayer. It shows they trust God.

Dear God,
be good to me.
The sea is so wide,
and my boat is so small.
(Fishers of Brittany, France)

DISCIPLE

Pray
Learn
Celebrate
Share
Choose
Live

What's the Word?

Jesus taught us to pray the Lord's Prayer. Part of this prayer is, "Give us this day our daily bread." When we pray these words, we are praying for the needs of all people. Draw some things that people need today.

Make it Happen

Finish this message to Jesus. As your friend and follower, I can

❑ share my toys.

❑ pay attention in school.

❑ say my prayers.

❑ help a friend.

❑ _____

(your own way)

Take Home

Share the stories about Jesus you have learned this week. Pray the Lord's Prayer together as a family. Talk about what the words mean.

105

CHAPTER TEST

Circle the correct answer.

1. The _____ of Jesus learned from him.

   teachers   followers

2. Jesus' followers believed that he was _____.

   the Son of God   an Apostle

3. Jesus taught his followers the _____.

   Sign of the Cross   Lord's Prayer

4. The _____ men Jesus chose to lead his followers were the Apostles.

   twelve   ten

5. Jesus _____ prayed to God the Father.

   never   often

 What did Jesus do to help his followers in the storm?

✝ We Gather in Prayer

Leader: Jesus, today we gather together to pray to you.

All: Jesus, we believe in you.

Leader: Jesus, you are wonderful.

All: Jesus, we praise you.

Leader: Jesus, you have done so much for us.

All: Jesus, we thank you.

Leader: Jesus, we want to follow you.

All: Jesus, help us to be your followers.

Jesus told his followers that he loved and cared for them.

WE GATHER

✝ *Jesus, help us to love and care for others.*

Look at the picture. What is happening?

WE BELIEVE

Jesus was a good teacher.
He wanted his followers to understand
what he was teaching.
He talked about things they knew about.

Read Along

One day Jesus was talking about shepherds.
He said, "I am the good shepherd, and I
know mine and mine know me." (John 10:14)

Jesus' followers knew all about
shepherds.
Shepherds stay with their sheep
night and day.
They take care of many sheep.
They know each of their sheep.
They do everything they can
to keep each one safe.

Jesus is our Good Shepherd.
He is with us night and day.
He knows each one of us.
He loves us very much.
He shows us ways to love
God and others.

Follow the path that shows ways to love God and others.

What signs did you follow along the way?

WE RESPOND

How is Jesus like a shepherd to us?

Many people gathered to welcome and praise Jesus.

WE GATHER

✝ *Jesus, we praise you.*

🏃 Imagine special visitors are coming to your school.
Act out how you will welcome them.

WE BELIEVE

Jesus visited many towns.
People welcomed him in different ways.
Some began to believe in Jesus.
They believed that Jesus was sent by God.

John 12:12–13

Read Along

Many people were in Jerusalem for a feast. They heard that Jesus was near the city, so they ran out to meet him. They waved palm branches in the air. They shouted,
"Hosanna!
Blessed is he who comes in the name of the Lord." (John 12:13)

As Catholics...

During every Mass we pray Hosanna. We pray the same words the people did when they welcomed Jesus to Jerusalem. We show that we believe Jesus is the Son of God.

At Mass next week, praise Jesus for all he has done for us.

Hosanna is a word of praise.
The people that day were happy to see Jesus.
They shouted Hosanna to praise him.
They waved palm branches, too.

WE RESPOND

When do you praise Jesus?

Show some ways we can praise Jesus.

Jesus taught in the Temple in Jerusalem.

WE GATHER

✝ *Jesus, we want to listen to your teaching.*

Where do you live?
Talk about the cities or towns that are nearby.
Do you ever go to these places?
Why?

WE BELIEVE

Jerusalem is an important city to Jews.
They go there for special feasts.
They go there to pray.

Jerusalem was very important in Jesus' time, too.
Jesus went to Jerusalem.
He taught the people there.

The **Temple** was the holy place in Jerusalem where the Jewish People prayed.

📖 Luke 21:37–38

Read Along

During the week before Jesus died, he taught in the Temple area every day. "And all the people would get up early each morning to listen to him." (Luke 21:38)

WE RESPOND

Where do you go to pray and listen to Jesus' teaching?

🎵 **In the House of Our God**

In the House of our God,
in the House of our God,
we give praise to the Lord
in the House of our God.

🤸 Make up actions for the song.

Jesus died and rose.

WE GATHER

✝ *Jesus, thank you for your great love.*

Think about the people who love you very much.
How do they show their love for you?

WE BELIEVE

Jesus showed his love in many ways.
He cared for people.
He listened to them.
He shared God's love with them.

Jesus showed his love in a special way.
Jesus died so that all people could live in God's love.

John 19:18, 25, 30, 42

Read Along

Jesus was nailed to a cross. Jesus' mother and a few followers were with him. Jesus died on the cross. After he died, some of his followers placed his body in a tomb.

On the third day after Jesus died, something wonderful happened.

📖 Matthew 28:1–7

Read Along

Early on Sunday morning, some women went to visit Jesus' tomb. They saw an angel sitting in front of the tomb. The angel said, "Do not be afraid!" (Matthew 28:5)

The angel told the women that Jesus had risen to new life. He told them to go tell the other followers.

Jesus died and rose to bring us new life. **Easter Sunday** is the special day we celebrate that Jesus Christ rose to new life. We pray Alleluia. Alleluia is another special word of praise.

WE RESPOND

How does your family celebrate Easter Sunday?

🏃 Celebrate what Jesus did for us. Color the Alleluia garden.

Easter Sunday the special day we celebrate that Jesus Christ rose to new life

Alleluia

Alleluia

Alleluia

PROJECT

Show What *you* Know

Match the sentence parts.

The Temple ●

● is the special day we celebrate that Jesus Christ rose to new life.

Easter Sunday ●

● was the holy place in Jerusalem where the Jewish People prayed.

Celebrate!

Circle the ways you can celebrate that Jesus died and rose for us.

Pray

Praise

Sing

DISCIPLE

Pray
Learn
Celebrate
Share
Choose
Live

Picture This

What does this stained glass window show?

Jesus is our

_____

- -

_____

Reality Check

The Church teaches us to respect all workers. People work in our neighborhood to protect and care for us. Who helps to protect and care for you?

❏ Police officers

❏ Firefighters

❏ People who keep my neighborhood clean

❏ People in my parish and school

Take Home

What are the two words of praise you learned in this chapter?

_____

_____

Say these words as a family.

117

Circle the correct answer.

1. The word people used to praise Jesus as he entered Jerusalem was _____.

   Hosanna   Alleluia

2. The _____ was the holy place in Jerusalem where the Jewish People prayed.

   Mountain   Temple

3. _____ died and rose to bring us new life.

   Jesus   Peter

4. _____ is the special day we celebrate that Jesus Christ rose to new life.

   Easter Sunday   Christmas Day

5. The city of Jerusalem was _____ in the time of Jesus.

   not important   very important

 Why did Jesus call himself the Good Shepherd?

Jesus Sends the Holy Spirit

10

✝ We Gather in Prayer

Leader: Let us celebrate that Jesus Christ rose to new life.

🎵 Sing for Joy

Sing and shout for joy, alleluia!
Sing and shout for joy, alleluia!
Sing and shout for joy, alleluia!
Alleluia! Alleluia!

Leader: Jesus wanted his followers to know that they would not be alone.

 Luke 24:36, 49

Read Along

Jesus did not want his followers to be afraid. He said to them, "Peace be with you." (Luke 24:36) Jesus promised his followers that he would send them a helper.

All: Jesus, thank you for sharing your peace and love.

Alleluia!

The risen Jesus visited his followers.

WE GATHER

✝ *Alleluia, Jesus is risen!*

Think of a time when someone surprised you. How did they surprise you? What did you do?

WE BELIEVE

Jesus wanted his followers to know that he had risen. So he visited them. Here is a story about one of his visits.

📖 John 21:2–12

Read Along

One night Peter and some of Jesus' other followers went fishing. They were on the boat all night, but they did not catch any fish. Early the next morning, Jesus' followers saw someone on the shore. The person called out. He told them to put their nets into the water again.

Jesus' followers put the nets back into the water. They were surprised when they saw the nets filled with fish. They suddenly knew that the person on the shore was Jesus.

Peter was excited. He jumped into the water and swam to shore. The other followers came in the boat. Jesus said to them, "Come, have breakfast." (John 21:12)

✶ Number these sentences 1, 2, 3, 4 to retell the story.

_3_ The followers knew the person was Jesus.
They went back to shore.

_4_ Jesus asked his followers to have breakfast with him.

_1_ Jesus' followers went fishing but did not catch any fish.

_2_ Someone on shore called out and told them to put their nets in again.
They caught many fish.

WE RESPOND

✶ Imagine that your class is having breakfast with Jesus.
Act out what you would say and do.

Jesus Christ promised that the Holy Spirit would come to his followers.

WE GATHER

✝ *Jesus, help us to remember you always.*

Think about your family and friends. Why do you like to be with them?

Share ways you can remember them when they are not with you.

WE BELIEVE

The risen Christ was going to return to the Father in Heaven. He did not want his followers to feel sad without him.

Jesus wanted his followers to remember him. He wanted them to tell others about God's love. He promised that the Holy Spirit would come to be with them.

The Holy Spirit would help Jesus' followers to:

- remember the things Jesus had said and done
- love others as Jesus had taught them
- tell others about Jesus.

After he made this promise, Jesus returned to his Father.

WE RESPOND

Ask the Holy Spirit to help you remember Jesus each day.

What is one thing you want to tell someone about Jesus?
Draw or write your answer here.
Who will you tell this to today?

The Holy Spirit was sent to Jesus' followers.

WE GATHER

✝ *Holy Spirit, be with us.*

Think of a time when you waited for someone to keep a promise. What did you do while you were waiting?

WE BELIEVE

After Jesus returned to Heaven, his followers went to Jerusalem. They stayed together in a house there.
They prayed and waited for the Holy Spirit.
Early one morning, Jesus' followers were together in one place. Jesus' mother, Mary, was with them.

Here is what happened when the Holy Spirit came to them.

Read Along

"And suddenly there came from the sky a noise like a strong driving wind, and it filled the entire house in which they were. Then there appeared to them tongues as of fire, which parted and came to rest on each one of them. And they were all filled with the holy Spirit." (Acts of the Apostles 2:2–4)

Pentecost is the day the Holy Spirit came to Jesus' followers. We celebrate Pentecost fifty days after Easter Sunday. On this day we celebrate the coming of the Holy Spirit. Every day we remember that the Holy Spirit is with us.

WE RESPOND

How do you think Jesus' followers felt on Pentecost?

Work with a partner. Make up a special tune or beat for this prayer.

You came on Pentecost.
You came to be with us.
Holy Spirit, we thank you
For coming to be with us.

As Catholics...

The Holy Spirit helps us to share God's love with others. God's love brings light and warmth to the world. This is why the Church often uses a picture of a flame or fire to remind us of the Holy Spirit. Fire gives us light and warmth.

Remember to pray to the Holy Spirit often.

The Holy Spirit is the Third Person of the Blessed Trinity.

WE GATHER

✝ *God the Holy Spirit, we love you.*

Look at the pictures.
What prayer do you think the children are saying?

WE BELIEVE

The Sign of the Cross is a prayer to the Blessed Trinity.

God the Father is the First Person of the Blessed Trinity.
God the Son is the Second Person of the Blessed Trinity.
God the Holy Spirit is the Third Person of the Blessed Trinity.

It is important for us to remember that the Holy Spirit is God.
The Holy Spirit is always with us.

Here is a prayer we say to praise the Blessed Trinity.
In the prayer, *glory* is another word for praise.

Glory be to the Father
and to the Son
and to the Holy Spirit
as it was in the beginning
is now, and ever shall be
world without end.
Amen.

WE RESPOND

Together think of actions to use when you pray these words of praise.

Pray this prayer together now with actions.

PROJECT

Show What you Know

Use the word shape to write the **Key Word**.
It is the day the Holy Spirit came to
Jesus' followers.

Pentecost

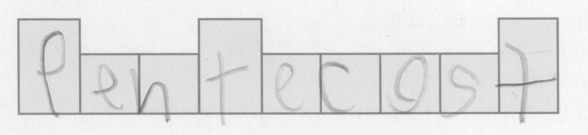

Pentecost

Reality Check

What can the Holy Spirit help
you to do today?

❑ Remember the things Jesus
said and did

❑ Love others as Jesus taught

❑ Tell others about Jesus

❑ Tell others about God's love

DISCIPLE

Pray
Learn
Celebrate
Share
Choose
Live

Picture This   Draw a flame of fire over each of Jesus' followers to remind you that the Holy Spirit came upon them.

Make *it* Happen

Name a prayer to the Blessed Trinity.

↳ **DISCIPLE CHALLENGE**

Say it.

Teach it to your friend.

Take Home

In many parishes, people join one another for breakfast after Sunday Mass. They talk with people they know. They meet new people. Check your parish bulletin or Web site to see if your parish does this. If so, plan to join in as a family.

129

Circle the correct answer.

1. Did Jesus visit his followers after he rose from the dead?

(Yes)   **No**

2. Did Jesus promise that the Holy Spirit would come to his followers?

(Yes)   **No**

3. Was Christmas the day the Holy Spirit came to Jesus' followers?

Yes   (No)

4. Is the Holy Spirit the Third Person of the Blessed Trinity?

(Yes)   **No**

5. Did Jesus want his followers to forget him?

Yes   (No)

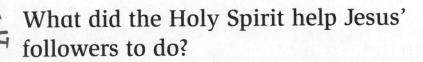 TALK ABOUT IT What did the Holy Spirit help Jesus' followers to do?

The Holy Spirit Helps the Church to Grow

11

✝ We Gather in Prayer

Leader: Holy Spirit, we know you are with us all the time. When we are excited or happy,

All: Holy Spirit, fill our ♡ with love.

Leader: When we are sad or lonely,

All: Holy Spirit, fill our ♡ with love.

Leader: When we feel strong or brave,

All: Holy Spirit, fill our ♡ with love.

Leader: When we are tired or afraid,

All: Holy Spirit, fill our ♡ with love.

The Church began on Pentecost.

WE GATHER

✝ *Jesus, we believe in you.*

Think about something exciting that happened to you.
Who did you tell about it?

WE BELIEVE

On Pentecost Jesus' followers were excited.
The Holy Spirit had come to them.
They left the house where they were staying.
They wanted to tell people what had happened.

📖 Acts of the Apostles 2:36–38, 41

Read Along

On Pentecost, Peter and the other Apostles told people about Jesus. Peter told the people to believe in Jesus. He asked them to become Jesus' followers. If they did this, they would receive the Holy Spirit.

That day about three thousand people received the Gift of the Holy Spirit. They became followers of Jesus.

This was the beginning of the Church.
The **Church** is all the people who believe in Jesus and follow his teachings.

Church all the people who believe in Jesus and follow his teachings

WE RESPOND

Why is Pentecost a special day?

🏃 Add yourself to the picture. Pretend you are in the crowd. Tell what you are seeing and hearing.

The first members of the Church did many things together.

WE GATHER

✝ *Holy Spirit, make us one in Jesus.*

🏃 Act out some things your family does together.

WE BELIEVE

The first members of the Church were like a close family.

They talked about Jesus' teachings. They learned together about ways to follow Jesus. They shared their money. They shared the things they had. They ate their meals together. They praised God together.

🎵 The First Church Members

("Here We Go 'Round the Mulberry Bush")

The first Church members shared
   their things,
shared their things, shared their things.
The first Church members shared
   their things
And we can do the same.

Sing this song again using these words:

The first Church members prayed
   together.

Together make up more
verses for this song.

WE RESPOND

How can you live like the first
Church members lived?

The Holy Spirit helped the Church to grow.

WE GATHER

✝ *Holy Spirit, help us to tell others about Jesus.*

Name some people who help you to believe in Jesus.

WE BELIEVE

The first members of the Church were filled with the Holy Spirit.

With the help of the Holy Spirit, they:

- believed in Jesus
- told everyone what Jesus had done for them
- shared God's love with others
- helped those who were poor or sick
- tried to be kind and fair to everyone.

Every day more and more people became members of the Church.

Q G A R M O S W

The Holy Spirit helps the Church to

_____ _____ _____ _____ .

👤 Read the sentence above.
What word is missing?
Circle every other letter.
Use the letters in the circles
to write the missing word.

WE RESPOND

Together the first members
of the Church prayed and
asked the Holy Spirit to be
with them.

Say a prayer to ask the
Holy Spirit to be with you.

As Catholics...

After the Church began, Paul
became a member, too. Like Peter,
he told everyone he met about
Jesus. Paul taught that all people
were welcome in the Church.

On June 29, the Church honors
Saint Peter and Saint Paul. On this
day, we remember that Peter and
Paul helped the Church to grow.

You can learn more about Saint
Peter and Saint Paul in the Bible.

The Holy Spirit helps the Church today.

WE GATHER

✝ *God, may we grow in your love.*

🎵 Share the Light

Share the light of Jesus.
Share the light that shows the way.
Share the light of Jesus.
Share God's spirit today.
Share God's spirit today.

WE BELIEVE

The Holy Spirit is always with the Church.
We are members of the Church.
The Holy Spirit helps us to know that Jesus loves us.
The Holy Spirit helps us to live as Jesus taught us.

With the help of the Holy Spirit we:

- pray
- share with others
- care for those who are poor or sick
- show respect for all people
- learn more about Jesus and the Church
- follow the rules when working and playing with others.

WE RESPOND

What can you and your family do to live as Jesus taught us?

🎵 Share the Light

Share the love of Jesus.
Share the love that shows the way.
Share the love of Jesus.
Share God's spirit today.
Share God's spirit today.

PROJECT

Pray
Learn
Celebrate
Share
Choose
Live

Show What *you* Know

Trace the **Key Word** in every faith statement.
Think about what it means.

The **Church** began on Pentecost.

The first members of the **Church** did many things together.

The Holy Spirit helped the **Church** to grow.

The Holy Spirit helps the **Church** today.

Fast Facts

Here are some ways to thank members of the Church all over the world.

thank you	English
kam sa ham ni da	Korean
dziekuje	Polish
gracias	Spanish
ahsante	Swahili
malo malo	Tongan

DISC1PLE

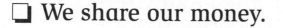

Reality Check

How are your family members like the first Church members?

- ❏ We talk about Jesus' teachings.
- ❏ We learn about ways to follow Jesus.
- ❏ We share our money.
- ❏ We share our things.
- ❏ We eat together.
- ❏ We praise God together.

Make it Happen

Make up prayer actions to the "Share the Light" song you learned. Then, teach it to your friend.

Now, pass it on!

Take Home

Make a poster with your family to show how the Holy Spirit is with the Church today. Use pictures from a magazine or draw your own. Write words to go with your pictures.

141

CHAPTER TEST

Circle the correct answer.

1. The Church began on _____.

Pentecost   Easter

2. The first members of the Church _____.

did not share   shared many things

3. The _____ is all the people who believe in Jesus and follow his teachings.

Holy Spirit   Church

4. The Holy Spirit helps us to live as _____ taught us.

the crowd   Jesus

5. The first members of the Church were _____ the Holy Spirit.

filled with   tired of

What does the Holy Spirit help us to do?

The Church Serves

12

✝ We Gather in Prayer

🎵 We Are the Church

We are the Church,
happy to be
the children in God's family.

We are following Jesus.
We are following Jesus.
Everyone old and young.
Everyone weak and strong.
We are following Jesus.

The Apostles led and cared for the Church.

WE GATHER

✝ *Thank you, God, for the Church.*

Some names have special meanings. Do you know any names with special meanings?

👤 Cross out every *N* to find the meaning of the name *Peter*. Then write the word you see.

N N R N N O N N C N N K N N

_____

WE BELIEVE

📖 Matthew 16:18

Read Along

One day Jesus asked Peter what he believed. Peter said he believed that Jesus was the Son of God. Jesus then said to Peter, "And so I say to you, you are Peter, and upon this rock I will build my church." (Matthew 16:18)

Before Jesus died, he asked the Apostles
to lead and care for all of his followers.
He chose the Apostle Peter to be the
leader of all the Apostles.

The Holy Spirit helped Peter and
all the Apostles to lead the Church.
Their belief in Jesus stayed strong.
They shared their love for Jesus
with others.

Peter and the Apostles went to
faraway lands.
They went to teach people about Jesus.
Many of these people became members
of the Church.
Peter and the other Apostles worked to
help the Church grow.

WE RESPOND

How can you share your love for
Jesus with others?

The bishops lead and care for the Church.

WE GATHER

✝ *Holy Spirit, please be with the Church.*

Think about your school.
Name some people who lead and
care for the students.

WE BELIEVE

Jesus chose the Apostles to lead the Church.
In later years, the Apostles chose other men
to lead the Church.

These men took the place of the Apostles.
They were the new leaders of the Church.
They did the work the Apostles had done.
They worked together to lead the Church.
These leaders became known
as bishops.

Bishops still lead and care for the Church today.
They teach about Jesus and the Church.
They pray with the people in their care.

Bishops take care of each diocese. A diocese is made up of many members of the Church.
A bishop leads and cares for the people of his diocese.

Look at the pictures on this page. Talk about ways the bishops are leading and caring for the members of the Church.

WE RESPOND

Who is your bishop?

Say a prayer and ask the Holy Spirit to help him.

The pope leads and cares for the whole Church.

WE GATHER

✝ *God the Father, bless the leaders of the Church.*

There are many people who are leaders. Match the leaders with the groups of people they work with.

a mayor • • a school

a principal • • a team

a coach • • a city

What are the ways these people work with others?

WE BELIEVE

The pope is the Bishop of Rome in Italy.
He takes the place of Saint Peter.
Just like Saint Peter, he leads and
cares for the whole Church.

The pope works together with all
the bishops.

- He prays for and takes care of
  the Church.

- He teaches what Jesus taught.

- He visits people all over the world.

- He helps people everywhere.

- He cares for those in need.

The Holy Spirit helps the pope to
be a good leader.
The Holy Spirit helps the pope to
care for the Church.

WE RESPOND

Imagine that the pope will be
coming to visit your city or town.
You have the chance to meet him.
What do you think he might say
to you?

Pope Francis

As Catholics...

The pope lives in the Vatican in
Rome, Italy. The main church
building of the Vatican is called
Saint Peter's. It is named for Peter,
the first leader of the Church.

People who are visiting from all
over the world gather outside
Saint Peter's every Wednesday.
There the pope speaks about Jesus
and the Church.

Find out the name of the pope.

The Church serves others.

WE GATHER

✝ *Jesus, help us love all the people of the world.*

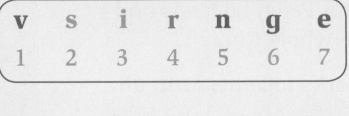

Use the code to fill in the correct letters.

v	s	i	r	n	g	e
1	2	3	4	5	6	7

___ ___ ___ ___ ___ ___ ___
2   7   4   1   3   5   6

is another word for caring and helping.

WE BELIEVE

Jesus showed his followers ways to serve others.
He fed people who were hungry.
He spent time with people who needed him.
He took care of people who were sick.
He shared God's love with everyone.

Jesus said, "As I have done for you, you should also do." (John 13:15)

Members of the Church serve others.
Look at the pictures on these pages.
They show members of the Church.
How are they doing what
Jesus did?

We show our love for God
when we serve others.

Which pictures show
how you and your family
can love and serve others?
Put a ♡ beside them.

WE RESPOND

What can you do in your
school to serve one another?

151

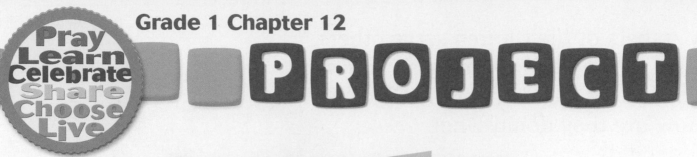

PROJECT

Show What *you* Know

Unscramble the words below. How have these people led and cared for the Church?

| plostAse | hopsib | oppe |

_____ _____ _____

------------------------ ------------------------ ------------------------

_____ _____ _____

Picture This

You are a member of the Church. Draw a picture of a way you can serve others.

Pray
Learn
Celebrate
Share
Choose
Live

Saint Stories

Blessed Teresa of Calcutta was known as Mother Teresa. She cared for people in India who were sick and homeless. She and her helpers fed people. They gave them a place to stay. Mother Teresa's helpers are called the Missionaries of Charity. They care for people in cities all over the world.

More to Explore

What is the name of your bishop?
What is the name of the pope? Find out!

Take Home

Talk with your family about ways you can serve others. Make a plan!

↳ **DISCIPLE CHALLENGE**
Print your family name on the pledge card. Ask each family member to sign it.

The _____ Family pledges to serve others.

_____

_____

_____

153

Circle the correct answer.

1. Did Jesus choose Peter to be the leader of the Apostles?

   Yes   No

2. Do we serve others by caring for and helping them?

   Yes   No

3. Is the pope the leader of your town?

   Yes   No

4. Do the bishops do the work the Apostles did?

   Yes   No

5. Does the pope only care about some of the members of the Church?

   Yes   No

 **TALK ABOUT IT** What are some ways the Church loves and serves others?

Come, Lord Jesus!
Be with us.

SEASONAL

CHAPTER 13

This chapter prepares us to celebrate the season of Advent.

WE GATHER

Think about a time your family was waiting to celebrate a special day.

What did you do?

How did you feel?

WE BELIEVE

The Church has a special time of waiting. Each year we wait for the coming of the Son of God. This waiting time is called Advent.

The word *Advent* means "coming." Each year during Advent we prepare. We get ready for the coming of God's Son, Jesus. We get ready to celebrate his birth at Christmas.

There are four weeks in Advent. The Church celebrates these four weeks in different ways. One way is by lighting candles on an Advent wreath.

On the Advent wreath there is one candle for each week. The light from the candles reminds us that Jesus is the Light of the World.

We pray as we light the candles on the Advent wreath. We remember that Jesus is with us. We prepare to celebrate his birth at Christmas.

Color the flames on each candle on the Advent wreath.

Ask Jesus to shine his light on all the world. Sing together.

🎵 **Advent Song**

Candle, candle burning bright,
shining in the cold winter night.
Candle, candle burning bright,
fill our hearts with Christmas light.

WE RESPOND

During Advent we can share Jesus' light with others. With your classmates talk about ways you can do this.

Write about or draw a picture of one way.

Bush
s

✠ We Respond in Prayer

Leader: Let us praise God and listen to his word.

Reader: Jesus said, "I am the light of the world. Whoever follows me will not walk in darkness, but will have the light of life." (John 8:12)

The Gospel of the Lord.

All: Praise to you, Lord Jesus Christ.

Leader: Jesus, help us to make the world bright with your life.

All: Come, Lord Jesus!

ADVENT

PROJECT DISCIPLE

Pray Learn Celebrate Share Choose Live

Picture This

Color by number.

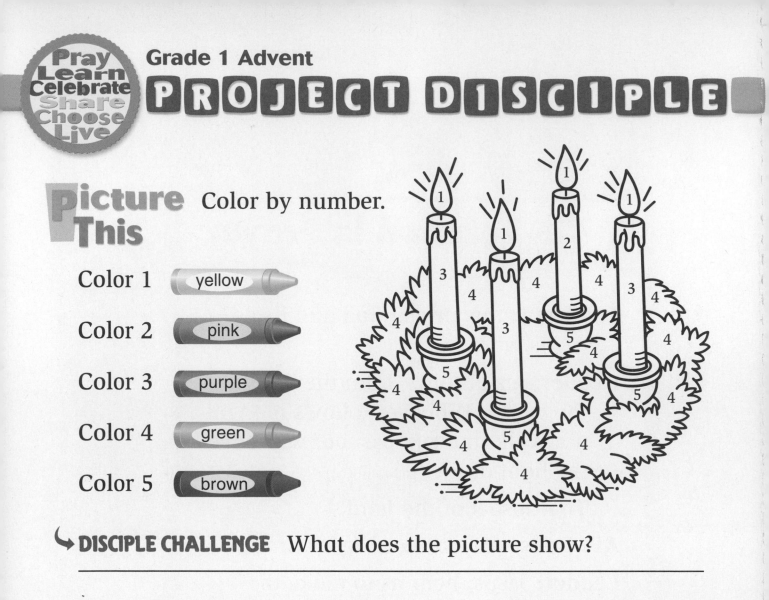

Color 1 — yellow

Color 2 — pink

Color 3 — purple

Color 4 — green

Color 5 — brown

↳ **DISCIPLE CHALLENGE** What does the picture show?

_____

- -

_____

Pray Today

Trace this prayer.

Pray it during Advent to show you are waiting for Jesus.

Come, Lord Jesus!

Take Home

How can your family share Jesus' light with others? Decide on one way and make it happen during the Advent season.

"For a child is born to us, a son is given us."

Isaiah 9:5

SEASONAL

CHAPTER 14

This chapter addresses the entire Christmas season.

At Christmas the Church celebrates the birth of Jesus.

WE GATHER

What do you think of when you think of Christmas?

WE BELIEVE

Christmas is a special time. During Christmas, we celebrate the birth of the Son of God. We celebrate God's greatest gift to us, his Son, Jesus.

Act out this Christmas play.

Narrator: Before Jesus was born, the ruler wanted to count all the people. Each man had to go back to the town his family came from to be counted. Joseph's family was from Bethlehem. So Joseph and Mary made the long journey to Bethlehem.

Joseph: Here we are, Mary! We're finally in Bethlehem! You must be very tired.

Mary: I'm all right, Joseph. It was a long journey. It will be so good to rest!

Joseph: Here is an inn. Maybe we can stay here.

Innkeeper: Not another traveler! What do you want?

Joseph: We need a place to stay.

Innkeeper: Sorry, there's no room left.

Joseph: Please, sir. My wife needs a place to rest. We're going to have a baby soon.

Innkeeper's Wife: We do have a place where the animals are kept. I put down fresh straw this morning. At least you can try to keep warm there.

Mary: Thank you for your kindness. May God bless you!

Narrator: So Joseph and Mary stayed there. Joseph made a place for the baby in the animals' feedbox. It is called a manger. He filled the manger with clean straw.

That night, Jesus was born. Mary and Joseph were filled with joy. They wrapped the baby in swaddling clothes and laid him in the manger.

Read Along

During Christmas, we sing with joy. Jesus has brought light and love into the world. He is with us now and forever.

Christmas is a time to honor the Holy Family. We remember the love of Mary and Joseph. We remember their love and care for Jesus.

WE RESPOND

Christmas is a time to share God's love with family and friends. Each thing you do for others can be a gift.

Color each gift box that shows a way you can share God's love. Then add your own way.

Each day during this time of year try to do these things.

Help keep my home clean.

Get along with everyone.

Pray for my family.

Share my things.

✝ We Respond in Prayer

Leader: Let us give thanks for the Son of God brings light and love into the world. Rejoice in the Lord always.

All: Rejoice in the Lord always.

Reader: Let us listen to a reading from the Bible.

> "The people who walked in darkness
>   have seen a great light;
> Upon those who dwelt in the land
>   of gloom
>   a light has shone.
> You have brought them abundant joy
>   and great rejoicing." (Isaiah 9:1–2)

The word of the Lord.

All: Thanks be to God.

🎵 **Joy to the World**

Joy to the world!
The Lord is come;
Let earth receive her King;
Let ev'ry heart prepare him room,
And heav'n and nature sing,
And heav'n and nature sing,
And heav'n, and heav'n and nature sing.

PROJECT DISCIPLE

Pray Learn Celebrate Share Choose Live

Fast Facts

During Christmas, many people use a nativity scene to remind them of Jesus' birth.

↳ **DISCIPLE CHALLENGE** Can you find the Holy Family in the nativity scene? Circle Jesus, Mary, and Joseph.

Question Corner

What are some ways your family celebrates Christmas?

- ☐ Exchange gifts to show our love
- ☐ Share special meals
- ☐ Decorate our home
- ☐ Pray
- ☐ Celebrate Jesus' birth
- ☐ Set up a nativity scene
- ☐ Go to Mass

Take Home

As a family, think of a special way you can share God's love with others during Christmas.

UNIT TEST

Fill in the circle beside the correct answer.

1. Jesus taught his followers how to _____.

    ○ pray   ○ read

2. Jesus told us that he was the _____.

    ○ pope   ○ Good Shepherd

3. The Church is all the people who believe in _____ and follow his teachings.

    ○ Peter   ○ Jesus

Circle the correct answer.

4. Is the Holy Spirit the Third Person of the Blessed Trinity?   Yes   No

5. Did Jesus choose John to be the leader of the Apostles?   Yes   No

6. Did Jesus' followers believe he was the Son of God?   Yes   No

continued on next page

Match each sentence to the correct picture.

7.

● Jesus invited people to be his followers.

8.

● Jesus taught his followers to pray.

9.

● The first members of the Church shared God's love with others.

10.

● The Holy Spirit came to Jesus' followers on Pentecost.

The Sacrament of Baptism

Part 1 I Open My Heart

Have you ever spent a day by the water? Make a postcard below. Use pictures and words to tell what the day was like.

You once had a very special day at the waters of Baptism. Baptism is a sacrament. A sacrament is a special sign given to us by Jesus. Baptism is the first sacrament that we receive. It welcomes us into God's family.

The Sacrament of Baptism

Part 2 We Come Together for Prayer

Leader: In Baptism, you became a child of God, a member of the Church, and a part of the Body of Christ. The waters of Baptism wash away sin and make us God's children.

Reader 1: "All you who are thirsty, come to the water!" (Isaiah 55:1)

Leader: Jesus, at the waters of Baptism, we became your brothers and sisters. Open our minds to think of you. (*Trace the cross on your forehead.*)

Jesus, at the waters of Baptism, we became your disciples, or followers. Open our ears to listen to you. (*Trace the cross on your ears.*)

Jesus, at the waters of Baptism, we became members of your Church. Open our mouths to speak the Good News. (*Trace the cross on your mouth.*)

Reader 2: "Baptism makes us members of the Body of Christ." (*Catechism of the Catholic Church,* 1267)

We are brothers and sisters in Christ. (*Join hands.*)

All: Jesus, make us one in you. Amen.

The Sacrament of Baptism

Part 3 I Cherish God's Word

"This is how all will know that you are my disciples, if you have love for one another." (John 13:35)

LISTEN to the reading from Scripture. Pay close attention to the reading.

REFLECT on what you heard. Think about:

- Your Baptism makes you a disciple of Jesus.

- How can you follow Jesus?

SHARE your thoughts and feelings with God in prayer. Speak to God as a friend.

CONTEMPLATE or sit quietly and think about God's Word in the Scripture passage from the Gospel of John above.

The Sacrament of Baptism

Part 4 I Value My Catholic Faith

Symbols help us to understand the Sacrament of Baptism.

Welcome those being baptized in your parish! Make a welcome poster together. Use the symbols of Baptism in your poster.

Symbols of Baptism

The Sign of the Cross shows that we belong to Jesus.

The baptismal water washes away Original Sin and gives us new life.

The anointing with oil is a sign of the Gift of the Holy Spirit.

The flame of the candle reminds us of the Light of Jesus Christ.

The white garment reminds us of our new life in Christ.

Catholic Identity Retreat

The Sacrament of Baptism

Part 5 I Celebrate Catholic Identity

In Baptism, you became Jesus' follower. Your good deeds bring joy to Jesus and show others that you are God's child.

Make a bracelet of beads to represent good deeds that you will do. This "good deeds beads" bracelet can remind you of your Baptism and your call to follow Jesus each day.

The **brown** bead is a reminder of the wood of Jesus' cross.

The **dark blue** and **light blue** beads remind us of the waters of Baptism.

The **yellow** bead is the color of Sacred Chrism.

The **white** bead is a reminder of the white garment.

The **orange** and **red** beads remind us of the flame on the candle. This light reminds us of the light of Jesus' love that guides us through life.

What good deed can you do each day? Share with your group.

The Sacrament of Baptism

Part 6 I Honor My Catholic Identity

(*All pray the Sign of the Cross.*)

Leader: Jesus, through Baptism, we became part of you, the Body of Christ. "Now you are Christ's body, and individually parts of it." (1 Corinthians 12:27)

Jesus, we will be your body on earth. We will live as you lived.

Reader 1: Our eyes are yours.

All: Help us to see with love and kindness.

Reader 2: Our feet are yours.

All: Help us to walk down good paths.

Reader 3: Our hands are yours.

All: Help us to bless others with our good deeds.

Leader: Jesus, we are yours.

All: Amen.

(*Adapted from a prayer by Saint Teresa of Ávila*)

Catholic Identity Retreat

Bringing the Retreat Home

The Sacrament of Baptism

Retreat Recap

Review the pages of your child's *Celebrating Catholic Identity: Liturgy & Sacraments* retreat. Ask your child to tell you about the retreat. Talk about the Sacrament of Baptism:

■ In Baptism we become children of God and members of the Church.

■ Through Baptism, we become Jesus' followers, or disciples.

■ We live out our baptismal call to follow Jesus.

Good Deeds

Part 5 of your child's retreat included a "good deeds" bracelet. Each night this week, have your child share with you any good deeds he or she did that day. Positively reinforce your child's actions. Plan a good deed you can do together as a family. Perhaps your family can volunteer to help at a local food pantry, shelter, or care center.

Take a Moment

Tell your child about the day of his or her Baptism. Show your child photos of the Baptism. Remind your child about his or her godparents and their role. Describe how the family celebrated the event. Begin a tradition of commemorating the anniversary of your child's Baptism.

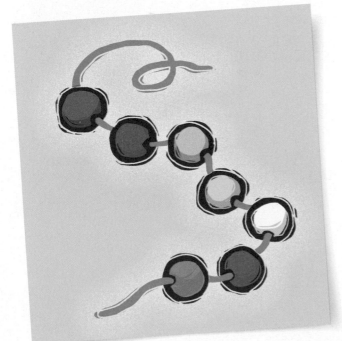

Family Prayer

At Baptism we pray the Baptismal Promises. This is when we respond, "I do," to a series of questions about our faith and our belief in the Blessed Trinity and the Church. Pray together that your family may always live these promises.

For more resources, see the *Catholic Identity Home Companion* at the end of this book.

Why We Believe
As a Catholic Family

What if someone asks us:

- Why does the Catholic Church baptize infants?

The following resources can help us to respond:

Baptism is the first sacrament that we celebrate. In Baptism, we are freed from sin, given the gift of God's life, or grace, and become members of the Church. No one is ever too old or too young to begin this new life in Christ. Many people are baptized as infants or young children. In this case, the parents and godparents take on the responsibility of raising this child in the faith. Others may be baptized as older children, adolescents, or adults. From the beginning, the Church has welcomed people of all ages into the Church through Baptism.

What does Scripture say?

"[The Apostle] Peter [said] to them, 'Repent and be baptized, every one of you, in the name of Jesus Christ for the forgiveness of your sins; and you will receive the gift of the holy Spirit. For the promise is made to you and to your children and to all those far off, whomever the Lord our God will call." (Acts of the Apostles 2:38–39)

"Jesus answered, 'Amen, amen, I say to you, no one can enter the kingdom of God without being born of water and Spirit.'" (John 3:5)

The Catholic Church's practice of baptizing infants demonstrates that God's grace is truly a gift, not something earned. The Sacrament of Baptism gives us new life in Christ and washes away all sin—in the case of an infant, this is the Original Sin with which all human beings are born; the infant does not first need to repent.

What does the Church say?

"The sheer gratuitousness of the grace of salvation is particularly manifest in infant Baptism. The Church and the parents would deny a child the priceless grace of becoming a child of God were they not to confer Baptism shortly after birth." (CCC, 1250; see Codex Iuris Canonici [CIC], can. 867 and Corpus Canonum Ecclesiarum Orientalium [CCEO], cann. 681; 686, 1)

"The custom of Mother Church in baptizing infants is certainly not to be scorned, . . . nor is it to be believed that its tradition is anything except apostolic." (Saint Augustine of Hippo [A.D. 354–430], great early Christian theologian and Doctor of the Church)

Notes:

We Belong to
the Church

Seasonal Chapters

PROJECT DISCIPLE

DEAR FAMILY

Pray Learn Celebrate Share Choose Live

In Unit 3 your child will grow as a disciple of Jesus by:

- appreciating the parish family and the ways the parish works and worships together
- celebrating God's love in the sacraments that Jesus gave us
- welcoming new members of the Church who receive Baptism
- choosing to act as "children of the light" by showing Christ to others
- understanding that God is always ready to forgive us and that he asks us to forgive others.

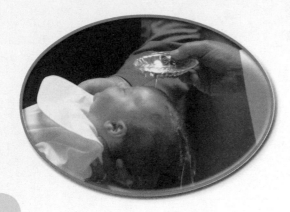

Question Corner Which sacraments have your family members received?

Baptism _____

Confirmation _____

Penance _____

Eucharist _____

Matrimony _____

Holy Orders _____

Anointing of the Sick _____

Give thanks to Jesus for all the sacraments.

170

Reality Check

The Christian family "is a community of faith, hope, and charity; it assumes singular importance in the Church."

(Catechism of the Catholic Church, 2204)

More to Explore

Chapter 15 focuses on the parish. Name your parish. What other parishes do you know about? You might check your diocesan Web site. Talk about other parishes you have belonged to and the parishes in the neighborhoods around yours. How does your parish work with other parishes? Help your child to feel the connections we all have as Catholics.

Make it Happen

Talk about God's love and forgiveness. Remind your child how important forgiveness is in our relationship with God and with others. Is there anyone you need to say "I am sorry" to? Is there anyone you need to say "I forgive you" to? Make it happen!

Take Home

Each chapter in your child's *We Believe* Grade 1 text offers a "Take Home" activity that invites your family to support your child's journey to more fully become a disciple of Christ.

Be ready for this unit's Take Home:

Chapter 15: Helping people who are hungry

Chapter 16: Singing at Mass

Chapter 17: Finding holy water in your parish church

Chapter 18: Praying to Jesus, the Light of the World

Chapter 19: Forgiving others in the family

We Belong to a Parish

✝ We Gather in Prayer

Leader: Jesus' followers said to him,
"Lord, teach us to pray." (Luke 11:1)
Let us join together and pray
the prayer Jesus taught.

All: Our Father, who art in heaven,
hallowed be thy name;
thy kingdom come;
thy will be done on earth
as it is in heaven.
Give us this day our daily bread;
and forgive us our trespasses
as we forgive those who
trespass against us;
and lead us not into temptation
but deliver us from evil.
Amen.

Our parish is like a family.

WE GATHER

✝ *God, thank you for the Church.*

🏃 Act out some ways families spend time together.

WE BELIEVE

We belong to the Catholic Church. We are Catholics. We belong to a parish.

A **parish** is a group of Catholics who join together to share God's love. They pray, celebrate, and work together. The people who belong to a parish are like a family.

We do many things with our parish.

- We praise and thank God.
- We share God's love with others.
- We learn how to be followers of Jesus.
- We work together to help people.

Key Word

parish a group of Catholics who join together to share God's love

WE RESPOND

What things do you like to do with your parish?

Finish the card.
Write your name and the name of your parish.

_____
I, _____,
belong to
_____
_____ Parish.

We gather together to worship.

WE GATHER

✝ *O God, we give you thanks and praise.*

🏃 Find out where these people are going. Connect the dots.

WE BELIEVE

Our parish joins together to celebrate God's love. We **worship** God. We give him thanks and praise.

Every week we gather to worship God in our parish church. Our parish church is a holy place. God is with us there in a special way.

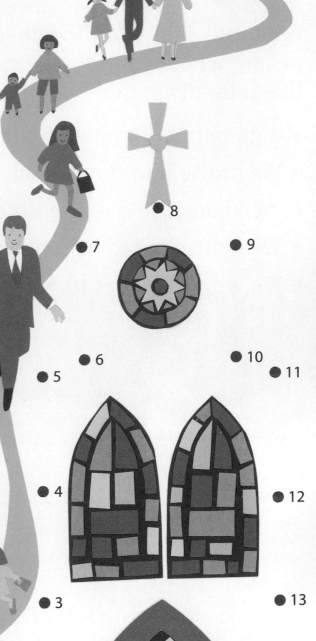

Key Word

worship to give God thanks and praise

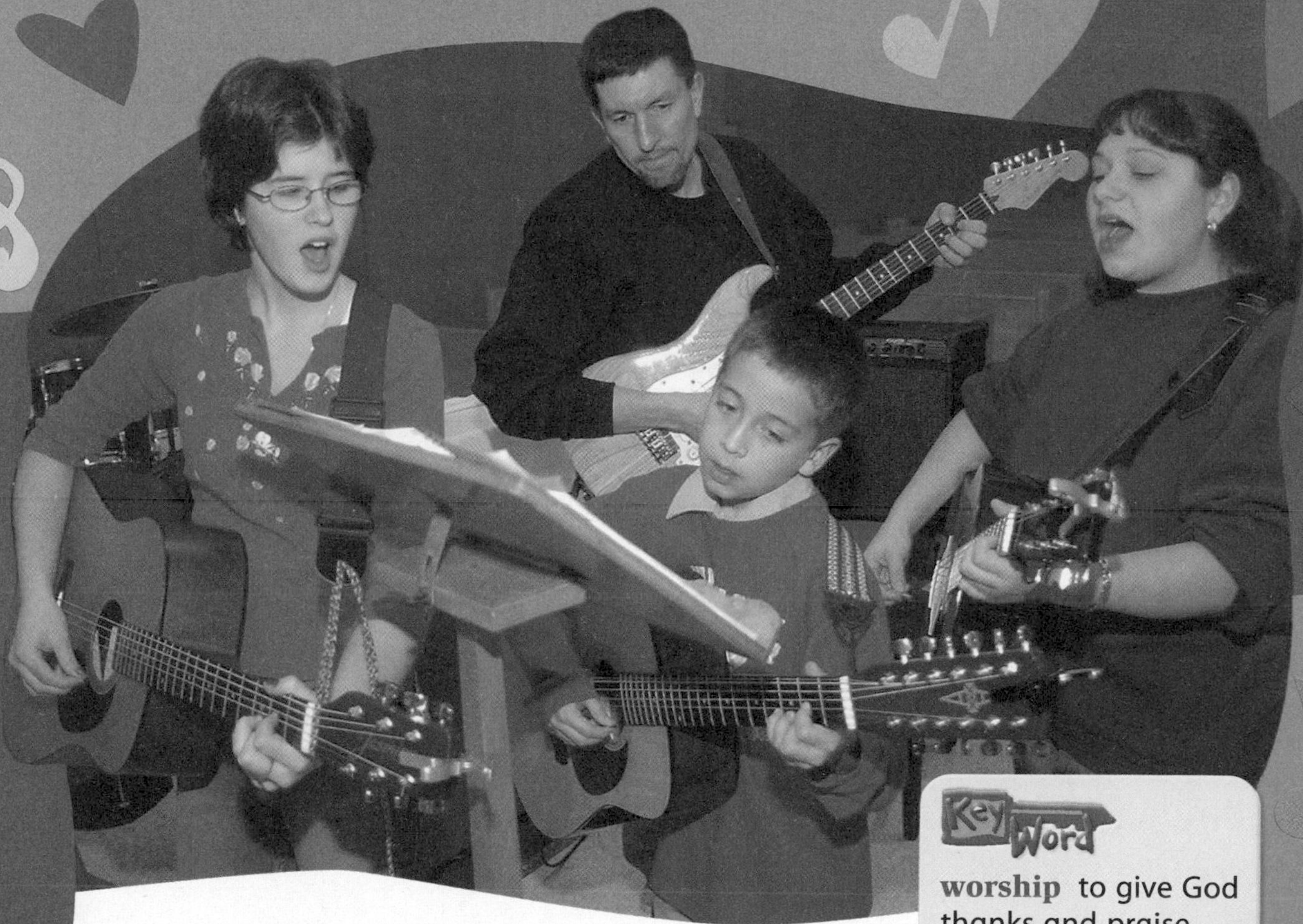

Look at the picture.
Talk about what you see.

WE RESPOND

How does your parish worship God?

♫ Open Our Hearts

God, we come to worship you:

Chorus

Open our hearts to listen to you.
Open our hearts to listen to you.

God, your love is always true:

(Chorus)

We work together as a parish.

✝ *Jesus, please help the members of our parish.*

Who are some of the people you know in your parish?

The leader of a parish is called the **pastor**. The pastor is a priest.

The pastor leads us in worship. He teaches us about Jesus. He helps us to care for one another.

 Who is the pastor of your parish? Write his name here.

_____

_____

Sometimes the parish has a deacon. He helps the pastor.

Other leaders in the parish work with the pastor, too. Together they help the parish family.

> **Key Word**
>
> **pastor** the priest who is the leader of the parish

Many people work together in our parish. Some help us to worship God. Some teach us about God. Some work with us to care for those who are sick or in need.

WE RESPOND

Talk about ways you thank the pastor of your parish.

Other people work in and help lead your parish. How can you thank them?

As Catholics...

Catechists teach the Catholic faith to the children, youth, and adults of the parish. They are very important people in the parish. They teach about Jesus and the Church. They help us to be friends and followers of Jesus.

Who teaches you about the Catholic faith?

Our parish helps many people.

WE GATHER

✝ *Jesus, help our parish to do your work.*

How would you help? Act out what you can do.

- Your friend forgot his lunch.
- Your sister spilled milk on the table.
- Your friend fell and got hurt.

WE BELIEVE

In our parish we help one another. We try to spend time with our parish family. We may join them for picnics or dinners. We help people of our parish who are in need.

Our parish helps other people, too. We gather food and clothes for those who are poor. We send money to those who are in need.

Our parish cares for those who are sick. People from the parish visit them. We can pray for them. We can also send them cards.

WE RESPOND

Circle one way you will help your parish this week.

- Join in singing and praying.
- Keep the parish buildings neat and clean.
- Pray for my parish.
- Be kind and friendly.

Together say a prayer for all those who are in need.

PROJECT

Show What *you* Know

Draw a line to match the Key Word puzzle pieces.

pastor

to give God thanks and praise

parish

the priest who is the leader of the parish

worship

a group of Catholics who join together to share God's love

DISCIPLE

Pray
Learn
Celebrate
Share
Choose
Live

Make *it* Happen

Think about the people in your parish. Answer each question.

Who helps you worship God?

Who teaches you about God?

Who cares for those who need help?

↳ **DISCIPLE CHALLENGE** Thank these people for the special work they do.

Reality Check

How is your parish like a family?

❏ We belong together.

❏ We help each other.

❏ We share God's love.

❏ We pray together.

Take Home

Some people do not have homes or jobs. These people need food. Many parish families join together to help people who are hungry. Some cook and serve meals to people who come to eat at a soup kitchen. Some collect food for the hungry. How can your family help people who are hungry?

CHAPTER TEST

Circle the correct answer.

1. Do the people in a parish pray, celebrate, and work together?

Yes   No

2. Is a parish church a holy place?

Yes   No

3. Is the president the priest who leads the parish?

Yes   No

4. Do the people in a parish help many people?

Yes   No

5. Do we forget about God when we worship him?

Yes   No

What do the people in your parish do together?

16

We Celebrate the Sacraments

✝ We Gather in Prayer

Leader: There are many signs of God's love for us. We see God's love in his gifts of creation and in one another. Jesus is the greatest sign of God's love. He shares God's life and love with us. Let us celebrate God's love for us.

🎵 We Celebrate With Joy

Chorus

We celebrate with joy and gladness
We celebrate God's love for us.
We celebrate with joy and gladness
God with us today. (Clap 2 times.)
God with us today. (Clap 2 times.)

God before us. God behind us.
God in everything we do.
God before us. God behind us.
God in all we do. (Chorus)

Jesus celebrated God's love.

WE GATHER

✝ *Jesus, you share God's life and love with us.*

What special times does your family celebrate?

WE BELIEVE

Jesus celebrated special times. He celebrated with his family and friends. He celebrated weddings and other family times.

Jesus celebrated Jewish feasts. He gathered with others to worship God. Together they celebrated God's love. They thanked God for his love and care. Together they prayed songs of praise to God.

Here is one of these songs of praise to God.

"Shout joyfully to the LORD, all you lands;
worship the LORD with cries of gladness;
come before him with joyful song."
Psalm 100:1–2

We can pray these words of praise.
Sometimes we pray them when we
worship God as a parish.

WE RESPOND

Pray together the song of praise
above. Make up actions for the prayer.

How else will you celebrate
God's love today?

We celebrate God's love.

WE GATHER

✝ *God, we praise you for your love.*

🏃 Pretend that someone your family loves is coming to your home. How will you celebrate this visit? Act out what you will say and do.

WE BELIEVE

We gather with our parish family to celebrate God's love. We gather to worship together.

When we worship, we thank God for sending his Son. We remember the things that Jesus said and did. We ask the Holy Spirit to help us.

When we worship, we use special words and actions.

🏃 Color in the letters of these special words we pray.

Alleluia
Amen

When we worship God together,
we do different things.
We ask God to be with us.
We pray using words, songs,
and actions.
We listen to God's Word.

WE RESPOND

What are some ways you
pray and thank God?

Stand and pray.

Alleluia. God, we praise you.
God, we thank you.
God, we love you. Amen.

Draw yourself worshiping God
with your parish.

Jesus gave us the sacraments.

WE GATHER

✝ *Jesus, thank you for giving us signs of God's love.*

Think about the people you love. How can you show them your love?

WE BELIEVE

God loves us very much. He loves us so much he sent his Son to us. Jesus, the Son of God, shares God's life and love with us.

Jesus wants each of us to share in God's life. So he gave us seven special signs of God's life and love. The seven special signs Jesus gave us are called sacraments. A **sacrament** is a special sign given to us by Jesus.

We gather with our parish family to celebrate the sacraments. Jesus is with us each time we celebrate.

WE RESPOND

Trace over the words in this prayer.

Jesus, thank you for the

sacraments.

Thank you for the

signs of God's life and love.

sacrament a special sign given to us by Jesus

The Church celebrates Seven Sacraments.

WE GATHER

✝ *Jesus, you are with us always.*

🎵 **Celebrate God**

Celebrate God with your hands.
Celebrate God with your voice.
Celebrate God in all that you do.
And God will be with you.

WE BELIEVE

The Church celebrates Seven Sacraments.
We receive the sacraments at different
times in our lives. But Jesus shares
God's life with us in each of the sacraments.
Each sacrament helps us to grow closer to God.

Look at the pictures. Each one shows
a sacrament that is being celebrated.

Baptism

Confirmation

Eucharist

Penance and Reconciliation

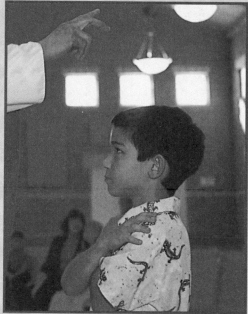

Anointing of the Sick

Matrimony

Holy Orders

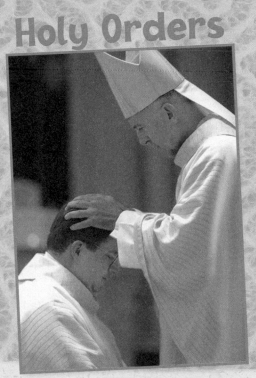

WE RESPOND

Talk about what is happening in each picture on these pages. Do these pictures remind you of things you have seen in your parish?

As Catholics...

We use the gifts of God's creation during the celebration of the sacraments. For example, water and oils are used to bless us. Light from candles reminds us that Jesus is with us. Bread made from wheat and wine made from grapes are used, too.

With your family, thank God for all he has given us.

Pray Learn Celebrate Share Choose Live

PROJECT

Show What *you* Know

Go back in your chapter and draw a [   ] around the  sacrament.

Picture This   Match the picture of the sacrament to its name.

● **Penance and Reconciliation**

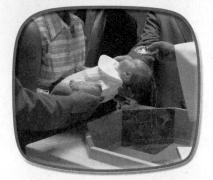

● **Matrimony**

● **Baptism**

DISCIPLE

Pray
Learn
Celebrate
Share
Choose
Live

Question Corner

Show this chart to friends and family members. Ask each person, "Which is your favorite way to celebrate God's love?" Each time someone names one of the actions, put a mark in the space below it.

sing	pray	listen	gather

DISCIPLE CHALLENGE Count up the marks in each box. Which action is the most popular?

Fast Facts

You can celebrate God's love at Mass every week.

Take Home

Some people use their talent to write songs of praise and thanks to God. We sing some of these songs when our parish family gathers to worship God. We sing these songs when we celebrate the sacraments. The next time you are at Mass, listen for these songs of praise and thanks to God. Join in the singing!

CHAPTER TEST

Circle the correct answer.

1. Jesus shares God's life with us in _____ of the sacraments.

each   some

2. _____ gave us the sacraments.

Peter   Jesus

3. The Church celebrates _____ Sacraments.

Seven   Ten

4. _____ is a special word we use when we worship God.

Hello   Alleluia

5. Jesus _____ gather with others to worship God.

did   did not

What are some of the special words and actions we use to worship God?

The Church Welcomes New Members

17

✝ We Gather in Prayer

Leader: God the Father,
All: We praise you.

Leader: Jesus, Son of God,
All: Show us how to live.

Leader: God the Holy Spirit,
All: Help us each day.

The Church welcomes new members at Baptism.

WE GATHER

✝ *God, we are your children.*

Look at the picture of the Stanik family. What do you think Father Marcos is saying to them?

WE BELIEVE

Father Marcos and the whole parish are welcoming the Stanik family. They are bringing their baby to celebrate the Sacrament of Baptism. The baby's name is Leo.

In Baptism, Leo will become a child of God. He will become a member of the Church.

Baptism is the sacrament in which we become children of God and members of the Church. Baptism is the first sacrament we receive.

> **Key Word**
>
> **Baptism** the sacrament in which we become children of God and members of the Church

When we were baptized, we became children of God. We became members of the Church, too. We celebrated Baptism with our parish family. They welcomed us into the Catholic Church.

As Catholics...

We receive the Sacrament of Baptism once. Some people are baptized when they are babies. Others are baptized when they are older. Older children, teenagers, or adults are usually baptized at a celebration on the night before Easter Sunday.

How old were you when you were baptized?

WE RESPOND

Why do you think Baptism is so important?

🎵 **We Are the Church**

We are the Church,
happy to be
the children in God's family.
(Repeat)

At Baptism we receive God's life.

WE GATHER

✝ *God, we want to grow in your love.*

 Look at the picture. What does the plant need so it can grow? Add to the picture what the plant needs.

Why is water important?

WE BELIEVE

Water is an important sign of Baptism. During the sacrament we are placed in water, or water is poured on us.

This happens in a special place in our parish church. This place is called the baptismal pool or font.

Water is a sign of the life God gives us. At Baptism God gives us a share in his life. We call God's life in us **grace**.

Grace helps us. It helps us to grow as God's children. It helps us to grow as followers of Jesus.

WE RESPOND

What would you like to say to God for his gift of grace?

Pray quietly now.

grace God's life in us

We say and do special things to celebrate Baptism.

WE GATHER

✝ *God, we celebrate your life and love.*

How can you welcome someone to your school?

What can you say and do?

WE BELIEVE

The Church celebrates Baptism with special words and actions.

Read Along

Leo's Baptism

Father Marcos talked to Leo's family about the celebration.

Father traced the sign of the cross on Leo's forehead. Leo's parents and godparents did, too. This showed that Leo would soon be a follower of Jesus.

Father placed Leo in the water of the baptismal pool three times. He said the words of Baptism:

Leo, I baptize you in the name
    of the Father,
and of the Son,
and of the Holy Spirit.

Each of us was baptized with water and these words, too.

WE RESPOND

What would you like to ask your family about the celebration of your Baptism?

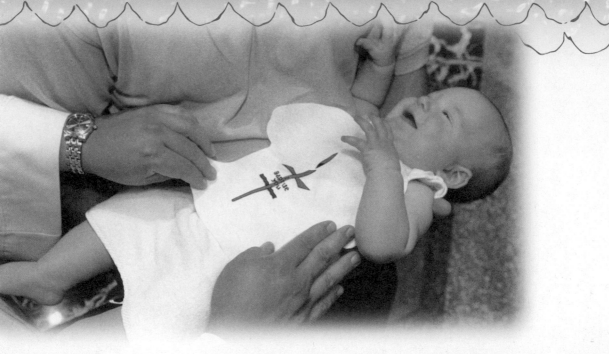

In Baptism we are joined to Jesus and one another.

WE GATHER

✝ *In the name of the Father, and of the Son, and of the Holy Spirit. Amen.*

Talk about what happened at the beginning of Leo's Baptism.

WE BELIEVE

These words and actions were also a part of Leo's Baptism.

Read Along

A white garment was put on Leo. Father prayed that Leo would always live as a follower of Jesus.

A candle was given to Leo's family. Someone from the family lit the candle. Father prayed that Leo would always walk in the light of Christ.

Everyone prayed the Lord's Prayer.

These same words and actions were part of the celebration of our Baptism.

As baptized members of the Church, we help one another to follow Jesus. We share in God's life together. We share our beliefs.

WE RESPOND

What will you do to live as a follower of Jesus?

Decorate this candle.

I will walk in the light of Christ.

PROJECT

Show What *you* Know

Use the **Key Words** to complete the puzzle.

Baptism
grace

1 Across: God's life in us

2 Down: The sacrament in which we become children of God and members of the Church

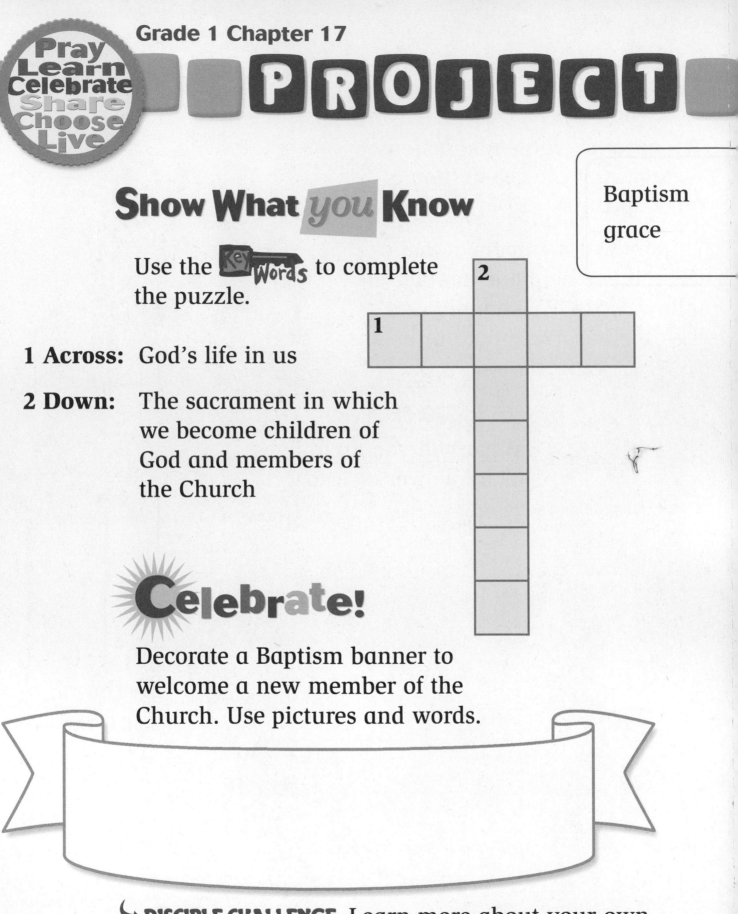

Celebrate!

Decorate a Baptism banner to welcome a new member of the Church. Use pictures and words.

↳ **DISCIPLE CHALLENGE** Learn more about your own Baptism. Ask your parents and godparents.

Pray
Learn
Celebrate
Share
Choose
Live

Picture This

Number the pictures of Leo's Baptism to put them in order.

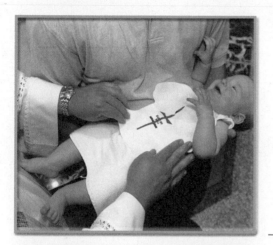

_____

_____

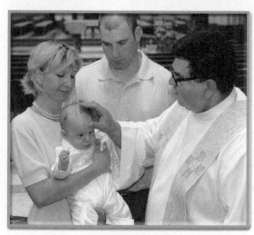

1

_____

Take Home

Holy water is water that has been blessed by a priest. The priest traces a cross over the water with his hand. He says a special prayer. Holy water is kept in a special container in church. With your family, find the holy water in your parish church.

Circle the correct answer.

1. Is Baptism the third sacrament we receive?

   Yes   **No**

2. Is water an important sign of Baptism?

   Yes   **No**

3. Do we become members of the Church in Baptism?

   Yes   **No**

4. Is grace God's life in us?

   Yes   **No**

5. Does the Church celebrate Baptism with special words and actions?

   Yes   **No**

 Why are we given a white garment and a candle at Baptism?

✝ We Gather in Prayer

Leader: Let us listen to the Word of God.

 John 8:12

Read Along

One day Jesus was talking to a crowd. He said to them, "I am the light of the world. Whoever follows me will not walk in darkness, but will have the light of life."

♫ Walk in the Light

Jesus is the Light for all:
Walk, walk in the light!
We follow him as we hear
      his call.
Walk, walk in the light!

Walk, walk in the light!
(Sing 3 times.)

Walk in the light
      of the Lord!

Jesus is the Light of the World.

WE GATHER

✝ *Jesus, we want to follow you.*

Think about things that give light.
How does the light of the sun help us?
How does a flashlight help us?
How do the lights in our homes help us?

WE BELIEVE

Read Along

"Jesus spoke to them again, saying, 'I am the light of the world. Whoever follows me will not walk in darkness, but will have the light of life.'" (John 8:12)

We believe that Jesus is the Light of the World. He helps us to see what God's love is like. He shares God's life with us.

Jesus wants us to follow him. If we follow him, we will have life with God.

WE RESPOND

What are some ways you can follow Jesus?

Draw a picture to show that Jesus is the Light of the World.

We receive the light of Christ.

WE GATHER

✝ *Jesus, help us to share your light.*

Think about someone who was kind to you.
What did the person do or say?
How did this make you feel?

WE BELIEVE

When we are baptized, we receive the light of Christ. We are told to "walk always as children of the light."

As children of the light, we are followers of Jesus. We:

- believe in Jesus
- act as Jesus wants us to
- love one another.

We show others the light of Christ when we:

- help our family and friends
- share what we have with others
- care about the way others feel.

WE RESPOND

How can you show others that you have received the light of Christ?

🎵 Walk in the Light

We walk together in Jesus' light:
Walk, walk in the light!
And let our own light shine so bright.
Walk, walk in the light!

Walk, walk in the light! (Sing 3 times.)
Walk in the light of the Lord!

Jesus asks us to share his peace.

WE GATHER

✝ *Jesus, we want to share your peace.*

Have you ever heard someone talk about peace? When?

WE BELIEVE

Jesus wanted his followers to be at peace. He wanted them to live in God's love. He wanted them to get along with one another. He wanted them to show love for one another.

📖 Matthew 5:1, 9

Read Along

One day Jesus went up a mountain. There he spoke to many people. He told them how to live as God's children. He said,
"Blessed are the peacemakers,
for they will be called the children of God."
(Matthew 5:9)

Jesus wants us to work for peace. A person who works for peace is a **peacemaker**.

We are peacemakers when we say and do kind things for others. We work for peace when we try to get along with all people.

peacemaker a person who works for peace

WE RESPOND

What will you do to be a peacemaker this week?

Act out one way you can share peace with one another.

213

We can make choices as children of God.

WE GATHER

✝ *Holy Spirit, help us as children of God.*

Think about some choices you made yesterday.
What games did you choose to play?
What did you choose for a snack?
What other choices did you make?

WE BELIEVE

God loves us very much. We are different from the rest of his creation. We are special. We can make choices.

We make choices everyday. Sometimes we make choices without even thinking about them. But God wants us to think about the things we say and do.

God asks us to choose to love him and others. He wants us to choose to do what Jesus taught us.

Here is a picture story. Circle the picture showing Tomás making a loving choice.

| Tomás wants to use his sister's . | Tomás can choose to just take the ball. | **OR** | Tomás can choose to ask his sister. |

WE RESPOND

Do you think it is always easy to make choices that show love for God and others? Tell why or why not.

Pray together now.

Holy Spirit, help us to make loving choices.
Help us to do what Jesus taught us.
Help us to live as children of God.
Help us to walk always as children of
the light.

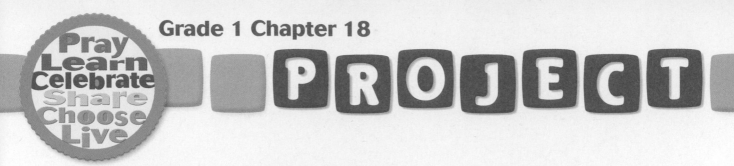
Show What *you* Know

Who is a person who works for peace?

_____

- -

_____

Picture This

On the candle write three ways that you can share the light of Christ.

DISCIPLE

What Would *you* do?

William and Rebecca are arguing in the playground. What could you do as a peacemaker? Add yourself to the picture.

More *to* Explore

Work with a friend. Who is a peacemaker in the world today? Write the person's name or draw a picture of the person in the heart.

Take Home

People all over the world gather to share Jesus' light by praying together. Sometimes people hold candles or other kinds of lights as they pray. Try this with your family. Gather together to pray. Use candles or other lights. As you pray, remember that Jesus is the Light of the World.

217

CHAPTER TEST

Circle the correct answer.

1. Is Jesus the Light of the World?

Yes   No

2. Do we show others the light of Christ when we tell lies?

Yes   No

3. Are we peacemakers when we fight?

Yes   No

4. Can we make choices to love God and others?

Yes   No

5. Do we receive the light of Christ at Baptism?

Yes   No

 Talk about ways we can work for peace at home, in school, and in our neighborhoods.

We Celebrate God's Forgiveness

✝ We Gather in Prayer

Leader: Holy Spirit, be with us now. Help us to think about ways we have or have not followed Jesus this week.

All: Holy Spirit, help us.

Leader: As I read these questions, pray to God quietly.

- Do I take time to pray?
- Am I kind to others?
- Do I listen to those who take care of me?
- Do I help people who need help?
- Do I tell the truth?

All: God, we are sorry for the times we have not loved you or others. Thank you for always loving us. We want to keep growing in your love.

Jesus told us about God's forgiveness.

WE GATHER

✝ *Jesus, thank you for teaching us about God's love.*

What is your favorite story?
Who is in the story?
What is the story about?
What happens at the end of the story?

WE BELIEVE

Jesus told stories to teach us about God's love and forgiveness. Here is one story he told.

📖 Luke 15:11–23

Read Along

A loving father had two sons. One day, the younger son asked his father for money. The son took the money and left home. He spent the money having fun.

Soon all the money was gone. The young man had nowhere to live and nothing to eat. He knew that what he had done had hurt his father. He wanted to go home and tell his father how sorry he was.

When the young man was near his home, his father ran out to meet him. He gave him a big hug. He was so glad to see his son again. The son told his father he was sorry. The father said, "Let us celebrate with a feast!" (Luke 15:23)

220

Number these sentences
1, 2, 3 to retell the story.

_____ When the son was near home, his father came to meet him. He hugged him. They celebrated with a feast.

_____ The son asked his father for money. The son left home. He spent all the money.

_____ The son knew that what he had done had hurt his father. He went home to tell his father he was sorry.

Jesus told this story to teach us that God always loves us. God is like the forgiving father in this story.

WE RESPOND

Why were love and forgiveness important in this story?

221

God is always ready to forgive us.

WE GATHER

✝ *God, you are our loving Father.*

🏃 Read the story about Tony. Act out what he should do next.

Tony's mom asked him to help his little sister tie her shoes. Tony said, "I don't feel like it." Then Tony thought about what he had said.

WE BELIEVE

We try to do things that show love for God and others. We try to follow God's laws. Jesus followed God's laws. He wants us to follow God's laws, too.

Sometimes we choose not to follow God's laws. We do things that do not show love for God and others.

Jesus taught us to ask God to forgive us. God always forgives us if we are sorry.

God is always ready to forgive you.
How does that make you feel?

🎵 **Children of God**

Chorus

Children of God in one family,
loved by God in one family.
And no matter what we do
God loves me and God loves you.

Jesus teaches us to love.
Sometimes we get it wrong.
But God forgives us ev'ry time
for we belong to the (Chorus).

Jesus wants us to
be sorry.
Sometimes we get
it wrong.
But God forgives us
ev'ry time
for we belong to the
(Chorus).

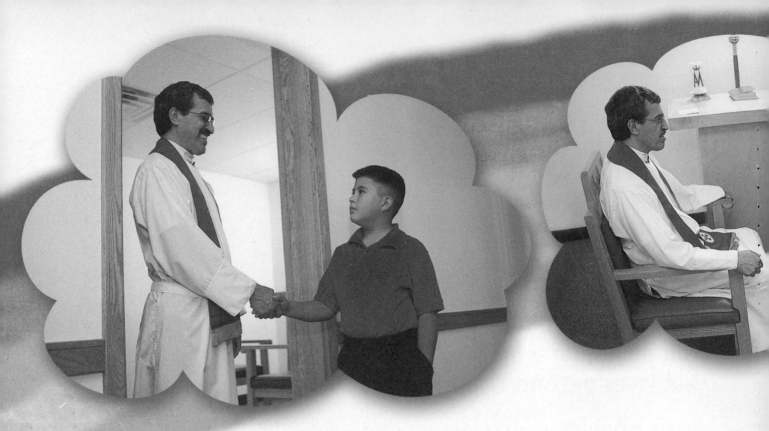

We celebrate God's forgiveness.

WE GATHER

✝ *God, thank you for your forgiveness.*

What are some ways to show others that you are sorry?

WE BELIEVE

When we make up with someone, we come back together again. This is called reconciliation.

We can always come back to God and ask for forgiveness. Jesus gave us a way to do this. It is the Sacrament of **Penance and Reconciliation**. We can call this sacrament the Sacrament of Penance.

In this sacrament we receive and celebrate God's forgiveness. We do these things.

- We think about what we have said and done. We are sorry for the times we have not loved God and others.

- We meet with the priest.

- We listen to a story from the Bible about God's forgiveness.

- We talk to the priest about what we have done. We tell God we are sorry.

- The priest shares God's forgiveness with us.

WE RESPOND

How can we tell God we are sorry? Talk to your family about God's love and forgiveness.

Penance and Reconciliation the sacrament in which we receive and celebrate God's forgiveness

We usually celebrate the Sacrament of Penance in our parish church. There is a special place in church where we meet with the priest. Here we can talk with the priest face-to-face, or we can talk from behind a screen.

Where is the Sacrament of Penance celebrated in your parish church?

Jesus asks us to forgive others.

✝ *Holy Spirit, help us to share God's peace.*

🏃 Look at the pictures.
Act out what you think is happening.

WE BELIEVE

When we celebrate the Sacrament of Penance, we receive God's forgiveness. We receive God's peace.

Jesus told his followers that it is important to forgive others. Jesus asks all of us to be forgiving. He wants us to share God's peace.

226

WE RESPOND

Ask the Holy Spirit to help you to be loving and forgiving.

Read the story.

Fran's little brother left her favorite book outside. It started raining. All the pages got wet.

Then Fran's brother said, "I am sorry, Fran. Please forgive me."

What would Fran say to be forgiving? Circle the words.

- "I am going to break one of your toys."
- "I loved that book, but I forgive you."
- "Go away. I do not want to talk to you."

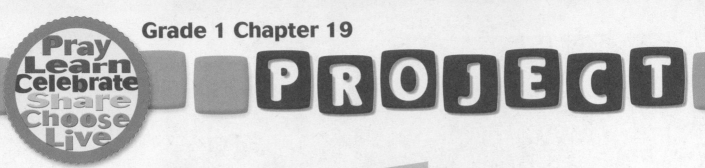

PROJECT

Show What *you* Know

Fill in the missing letters to read
an important message.

I can receive and celebrate God's forgiveness in the
Sacrament of

__ e __ a __ c __ a ____

__ e __ o __ __ i __ ia __ io __ .

Reality Check

Check your favorite way to tell
someone you are sorry.

❏ Please forgive me.

❏ I am sorry.

❏ I apologize for what I did.

↳ **DISCIPLE CHALLENGE** Remember
to tell God and others when
you are sorry.

DISCIPLE

Make *it* Happen

Write a forgiveness picture story in the space below. Be sure to include a beginning, a middle, and an end to your story.

beginning	middle	end

Take Home

Invite your family to make a chart at home that tallies the number of times family members forgive each other. When someone forgives, he or she puts a checkmark on the chart.

229

Circle the correct answer.

1. Jesus told stories about God's love and _____.

forgetting   forgiveness

2. In one of Jesus' stories God is like the _____.

son   forgiving father

3. God is _____ ready to forgive us.

always   sometimes

4. In the Sacrament of Penance, we _____ and celebrate God's forgiveness.

receive   return

5. It is _____ to forgive others.

not important   important

What are some things we do when we celebrate the Sacrament of Penance?

A good samaritan

"Try to learn what is pleasing to the Lord."

Ephesians 5:10

SEASONAL

CHAPTER 20

This chapter offers preparation for the season of Lent.

The Church gets ready to celebrate Jesus' Death and Resurrection.

WE GATHER

When do you remember what your family has done for you? When do you remember what God has done for you?

WE BELIEVE

Lent is a special time in the Church. We remember all that Jesus has done for us. We get ready for the Church's great celebration of Jesus' Death and Resurrection.

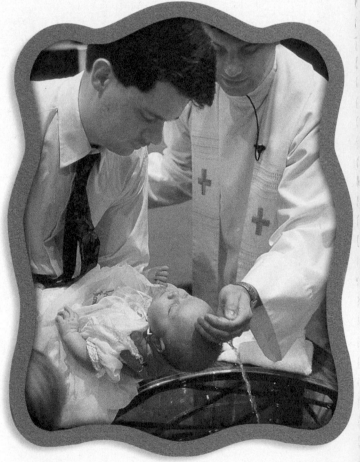

Lent is a time to remember our Baptism. In Baptism we first received grace, the gift of God's life. During Lent we praise Jesus for sharing his life with us.

We were baptized in the name of the Father, and of the Son, and of the Holy Spirit. Praying the Sign of the Cross reminds us of our Baptism.

Talk about the special things that happened at your Baptism.

Close your eyes. Thank Jesus for sharing his life with you. Now pray together the Sign of the Cross.

During Lent we try to grow closer to Jesus. We pray and follow his example. We thank God for his great love. We celebrate God's forgiveness. We help people who are sick, hungry, and lonely.

Followers of Jesus Christ should always do these things. However, they have special meaning when we do them during Lent.

Look at the pictures on this page. Act out what the people in the pictures are doing and saying.

WE RESPOND

Each time you do something to grow closer to Jesus during Lent, color one of the spaces in this cross.

✝ We Respond in Prayer

Leader: The Lord calls us to days of quiet time, prayer, and kind acts. Blessed be the name of the Lord.

All: Now and for ever.

Leader: During this time of Lent we trust in God's love and forgiveness.

All: Happy are those who trust in the Lord.

Leader: Together we pray as Jesus taught us.

All: Our Father, who art in heaven,
hallowed be thy name;
thy kingdom come;
thy will be done on earth as it is
in heaven.
Give us this day our daily bread;
and forgive us our trespasses
as we forgive those who trespass
against us;
and lead us not into temptation,
but deliver us from evil.
Amen.

PROJECT DISCIPLE

Pray
Learn
Celebrate
Share
Choose
Live

Celebrate!

Draw yourself doing something that brings you closer to Jesus during Lent.

Pray Today

Finish this prayer.

Jesus, thank you for sharing your

_____

- -

_____ .

Thank you for giving me

_____

- -

_____ .

Amen.

Take Home

Talk about ways your family can grow closer to Jesus during Lent.

Plan to make one of these ways happen.

Lord, through your cross you brought joy to the world.

This chapter includes the three days from Holy Thursday evening until Easter Sunday.

The Church celebrates that Jesus died and rose to new life.

WE GATHER

Think about the crosses that you see. How are they different?

WE BELIEVE

Lent is a time to prepare for the Church's greatest celebration. Lent gets us ready for the great Three Days called the Easter Triduum. We celebrate Jesus' dying and rising to new life.

During the Three Days, we gather with our parish. We celebrate at night and during the day.

We do the things Jesus asked us to do. We remember that Jesus gave himself to us at the Last Supper. We remember the ways Jesus loved and served others.

We listen to readings from the Bible. We pray before the cross. The cross reminds us of Jesus' dying and rising to new life.

✞ Draw a picture here to show one way you will celebrate the Three Days with your parish.

239

We sing with joy to celebrate that Jesus rose from the dead. We remember our Baptism in a special way. We welcome new members into the Church. We celebrate with songs of joy and praise.

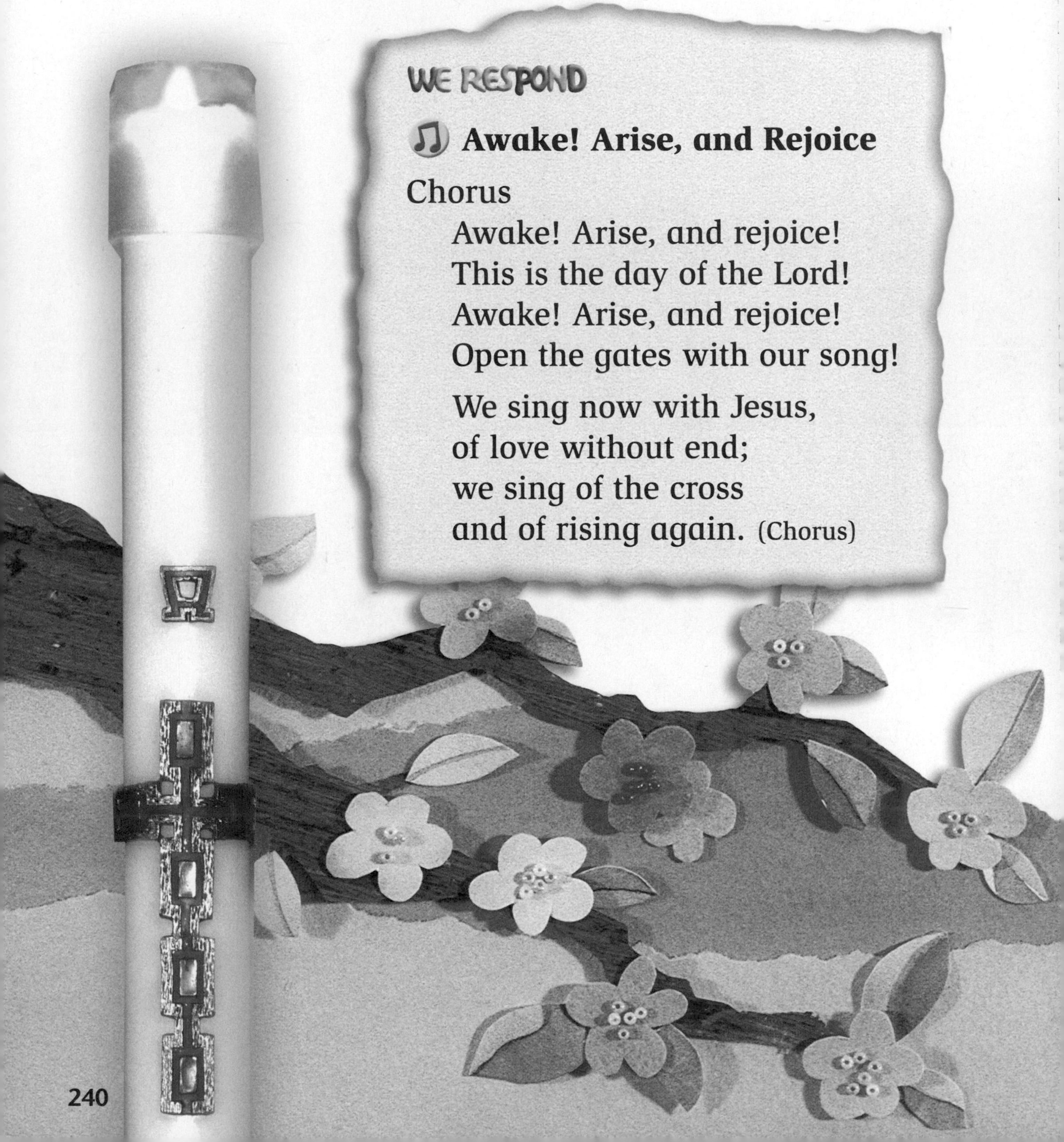

WE RESPOND

♫ Awake! Arise, and Rejoice

Chorus

Awake! Arise, and rejoice!
This is the day of the Lord!
Awake! Arise, and rejoice!
Open the gates with our song!

We sing now with Jesus,
of love without end;
we sing of the cross
and of rising again. (Chorus)

✝ We Respond in Prayer

Leader: Lord, through your cross
you brought joy to the world.

All: Lord, through your cross
you brought joy to the world.

Leader: Holy is God!

All: Holy is God!

Leader: Holy and strong!

All: Holy and strong!

🎵 **Shout from the Mountains**

And we sing:
Holy, holy,
holy is God!
Holy, holy,
holy and strong!

Celebrate!

Match the pictures to the ways that we can celebrate the Three Days.

● Pray before the cross.

● Remember that Jesus gave himself to us.

● Remember our Baptism.

Take Home

Mark the Three Days on your family calendar. Remember to celebrate with your parish on these days.

Draw a line to match the sentence parts.

1. Jesus is   ●   ● we use special words and actions.

2. Every week our parish gathers   ●   ● are called sacraments.

3. When we worship   ●   ● we become members of the Church.

4. The seven special signs Jesus gave us   ●   ● to worship God.

5. When we are baptized   ●   ● the Light of the World.

continued on next page

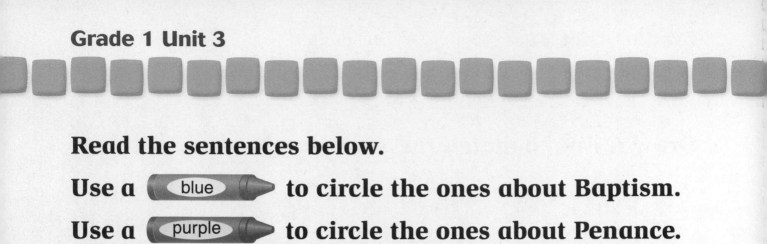

Read the sentences below.

Use a [blue] to circle the ones about Baptism.

Use a [purple] to circle the ones about Penance.

6. We are welcomed to the Church.

7. We tell God we are sorry.

8. We are invited to walk in the light of Christ.

9. Water is a sign of the life God gives us.

10. The priest shares God's forgiveness with us.

Serving Others

Part 1 I Open My Heart

We follow Jesus when we love and care for one another. Look at the picture. How does it show caring for others?

Think about times at school, with friends, or with your family. In what ways do you love and care for others? Role-play one of these ways.

Serving Others

Part 2 We Come Together for Prayer

Leader: Listen to God's Word.

Jesus said, "As I have done for you, you should also do" (John 13:15).

Think about ways that Jesus served others.

Jesus told us to follow his example. Jesus, thank you for loving us. Help us to follow your example.

All: Jesus, you gave me 🖐 to serve like you.

Jesus, you gave me a 👄 to speak kind words like you.

Jesus, you gave me a ❤ to love like you.

Leader: How can you serve like Jesus? (*All complete the prayer below.*)

Jesus, I want to follow your example.

Help me to serve by: _____

_____

All: Jesus, help us to show your love in all we do. Amen.

Serving Others

Part 3   I Cherish God's Word

Jesus said, "Whoever wishes to be great among you shall be your servant" (Matthew 20:26).

LISTEN to the reading from Scripture. Pay close attention to the reading.

REFLECT on what you heard. Think about:

- A servant is a person who serves others. Think of people who show love by serving others. What makes those who serve others "great," as Jesus says?

SHARE your thoughts and feelings with God in prayer. Speak to God as a friend.

CONTEMPLATE or sit quietly and think about God's Word in the Scripture passage from the Gospel of Matthew above.

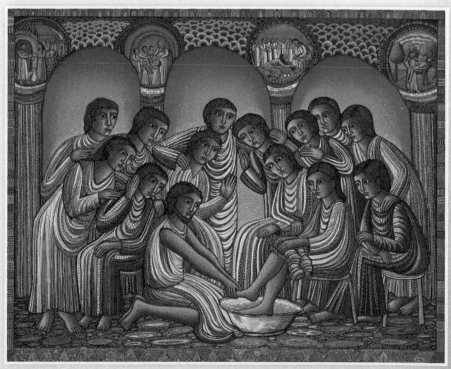

Washing of the Feet, by John August Swanson

Serving Others

Part 4   I Value My Catholic Faith

Saint Teresa of Calcutta followed Jesus by serving the poor. She helped people who had no homes. She opened schools for children. She cared for people who were sick. She said, "Do small things with great love." Even the little things we do each day can make a difference to others.

Draw one way you can serve others. You will share your drawings as a group.

Saint Teresa of Calcutta, holding a child, at her mission in Calcutta, India, in 1980

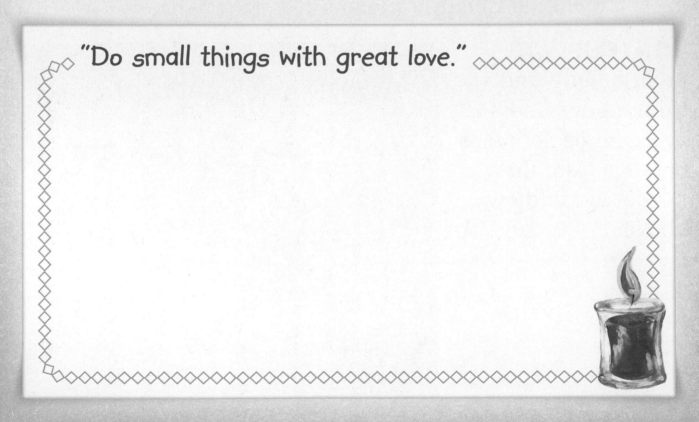

"Do small things with great love."

Catholic Identity Retreat

Serving Others

Part 5   I Celebrate Catholic Identity

"Let us not grow tired of doing good." (Galatians 6:9)

What are some of the needs that you are concerned about in your parish or community? Talk about these needs together. Then make an announcement for the parish bulletin. Ask people to be aware of these needs and to respond.

✝ Parish Bulletin ✝

Serving Others

Part 6   I Honor My Catholic Identity

Leader: Jesus, help us to show your love. When we are at school,

All: help us to show your love.

Leader: When we are with our friends,

All: help us to show your love.

Leader: When we are with our families,

All: help us to show your love.

Leader: Together, let us pray an Act of Love.

All: O God, we love you above all things. Help us to love ourselves and one another as Jesus taught us to do. Amen.

Catholic Identity Retreat

Bringing the Retreat Home

Serving Others

Retreat Recap

Review the pages of your child's *Celebrating Catholic Identity: Morality* retreat. Ask your child to tell you about the retreat. Talk about serving others:

■ Jesus lived a life of service.

■ Jesus taught us to follow him by serving others.

■ Even the little things we do each day can make a difference in others' lives.

Small Things, Great Love

Review together the saying from Part 4 of the retreat: "Do small things with great love." Make a household list of "small" everyday things your family can do for each other with great love—ordinary acts such as cleaning up, taking out garbage, making a meal, and so on—and carry these out this week.

To-Do List

☐ _____

☐ _____

☐ _____

☐ _____

☐ _____

☐ _____

Take a Moment

In Part 5 your child wrote an announcement about needs in the parish or community. Talk about ways your family might respond to those needs. Choose one together and make a plan to do it.

Family Prayer

Pray this together at mealtime or bedtime:

May we always give ourselves cheerfully for the glory of your name and the service of our neighbor, through Christ our Lord.

(Based on the Prayer over the Offerings, Memorial of Saint Philip Neri)

For more resources, see the *Catholic Identity Home Companion* at the end of this book.

Catholic Identity Retreat

Why We Believe
As a Catholic Family

What if someone asks us:

- What is Catholic social teaching?
- Where does Catholic social teaching come from?

The following resources can help us to respond:

Jesus' entire life was one of service. Jesus' life and teaching are the foundation of Catholic social teaching. By his example and by everything he taught, Jesus upheld the dignity and rights of every human person. Human dignity is the value and worth that come from being created in God's image and likeness.

There are seven themes of Catholic social teaching:

1. Life and Dignity of the Human Person

2. Call to Family, Community, and Participation

3. Rights and Responsibilities of the Human Person

4. Option for the Poor and Vulnerable

5. Dignity of Work and the Rights of Workers

6. Solidarity of the Human Family

7. Care for God's Creation

🌿 What does Scripture say?

Jesus said, "For I was hungry and you gave me food, I was thirsty and you gave me drink, a stranger and you welcomed me, naked and you clothed me, ill and you cared for me, in prison and you visited me" (Matthew 25:35–36).

"If someone who has wordly means sees a brother in need and refuses him compassion, how can the love of God remain in him?" (1 John 3:17)

Catholic social teaching calls us to work for justice and peace as Jesus did. We are encouraged to work for change in policies and laws so that the dignity and freedom of every person may be respected.

🌿 What does the Church say?

"How can we not recognize Lazarus, the hungry beggar in the parable (cf. Lk 17:19-31), in the multitude of human beings without bread, a roof or a place to stay? How can we fail to hear Jesus: 'As you did it not to one of the least of these, you did it not to me' (Mt 25:45)?" (CCC, 2463)

"Human society . . . demands that men be guided by justice, respect the rights of others and do their duty."
(Saint John XXIII, *Pacem in Terris* ("Peace on Earth"), 35)

Notes:

We Celebrate and Live Our Faith

Seasonal Chapter

DEAR FAMILY

In Unit 4 your child will grow as a disciple of Jesus by:

- appreciating that at Mass we celebrate what Jesus did at the Last Supper
- gathering with the parish family for the celebration of the Mass
- sharing God's love by loving and serving our family and others
- honoring Mary and all the saints by asking them to pray for us and by following their example
- caring for all of God's creation, and respecting all people as Jesus taught us to do.

Saint Stories

Introduce your child to Saint Jerome who is the Patron of Scripture Scholars. As a young student, he learned Latin and Greek and later translated the Bible into Latin. He said, "Now we must translate the words of Scripture into deeds, and instead of speaking holy words, we must do them." What words of Scripture can you do today? Pray to Saint Jerome before the Liturgy of the Word at Mass this Sunday.

Celebrate!

In Chapter 22, your child is reminded of the Third Commandment, "Remember to keep holy the Lord's Day." Participating in the Sunday celebration of the Mass is the first way we keep the Lord's Day holy. We can also spend time together as a family and do something for those in need. Plan to make this Sunday holy by doing all of these!

Reality Check

"Parents should initiate their children at an early age into the mysteries of the faith of which they are the 'first heralds' for their children."

(*Catechism of the Catholic Church*, 2225)

Picture This

Chapter 23 has many photos of what happens at Mass. Look at the pictures together, and ask your child about what is happening in each one. How are the photos like what happens at your parish? How are they different?

Show That You Care

At the end of Mass, we often hear these words: "Go in peace." What are some ways in which your family shows love for the Lord and serves him? Choose one special way you will love and serve the Lord this week.

Take Home

Each chapter in your child's *We Believe* Grade 1 text offers a "Take Home" activity that invites your family to support your child's journey to more fully become a disciple of Christ.

Be ready for this unit's Take Home:

Chapter 22: Listing people who help us worship at Mass

Chapter 23: Praying for parishioners who are sick

Chapter 24: Sharing God's love as a family

Chapter 25: Making a family tree

Chapter 26: Caring for God's creation

Jesus Gives Us the Eucharist

✝ We Gather in Prayer

Leader: Let us join hands and form a circle of friends.

Reader 1: O God, we gather now to pray.

All: We praise you together.

Reader 2: We listen to your Word.

All: We praise you together.

Reader 3: We lift up our hearts.

All: We praise you together.

Reader 4: We share your love with everyone.

All: We praise you together.

Jesus shared a special meal with his Apostles.

WE GATHER

✝ *God, let us share in your life.*

🧍 Think about a holiday celebration. Here are some things you do to celebrate. Finish the sentences using these words.

friends	meal	God	family

Gather your __ __ __ __ __ __.

Invite __ __ __ __ __ __ __.

Have a __ __ __ __ together.

Thank __ __ __ for this special time.

WE BELIEVE

On the night before he died, Jesus was with his Apostles in Jerusalem. They had gathered for a Jewish holiday. They were celebrating with a special meal. Jesus told them that he loved them.

Here is what Jesus said and did.

📖 Matthew 26:26–28

Read Along

While they were eating, Jesus picked up the bread. He blessed it and broke it. He gave it to his friends. He said, "Take and eat; this is my body." (Matthew 26:26)

Then Jesus took a cup of wine. He gave God thanks. He passed the cup to his friends and said, "Drink from it, all of you, for this is my blood." (Matthew 26:27–28)

We call this last meal Jesus shared with his Apostles the Last Supper. Jesus gave his Apostles the gift of himself. The bread and wine became the Body and Blood of Jesus.

WE RESPOND

Imagine you are at the Last Supper. How do you think Jesus' followers feel? How do you think Jesus feels? How do you feel?

We celebrate what Jesus said and did at the Last Supper.

WE GATHER

✝ *Jesus, we remember what you have done for us.*

Here are some ways to remember special times.

- Talk about them with friends and family.
- Take pictures or videos and look at them later.
- Celebrate them again and again.

WE BELIEVE

Jesus told his Apostles to remember what he said and did at the Last Supper.

The Church does this at the celebration of the Eucharist. Together we celebrate what Jesus said and did at the Last Supper.

The **Eucharist** is the sacrament of the Body and Blood of Jesus Christ. In this sacrament, the bread and wine become the Body and Blood of Jesus Christ.

Eucharist the sacrament of the Body and Blood of Jesus Christ

The word *eucharist* means "to give thanks." At the celebration of the Eucharist, we thank God for his many gifts. We thank Jesus for all he has done for us.

WE RESPOND

Pray quietly. Think of all the things Jesus has done for us.

 Finish this prayer.

Thank you, Jesus, for

_____

_____

_____

We celebrate the Sacrament of the Eucharist.

WE GATHER

✝ *Jesus, thank you for the gift of yourself in the Eucharist.*

When do we worship God? What are some ways we praise and thank him?

WE BELIEVE

The **Mass** is another name for the celebration of the Eucharist. The Mass is the Church's greatest celebration.

At Mass we worship God together. We praise the Father for his love. We celebrate the life of his Son, Jesus. We ask the Holy Spirit to help us celebrate.

Key Word

Mass another name for the celebration of the Eucharist

Jesus is with us in a special way at Mass. He is with us when we gather together. He is with us when we listen to God's Word.

Jesus is with us when we remember what he said and did at the Last Supper. He is with us when we share his Body and Blood.

WE RESPOND

Jesus is with us always. He is with us in a special way when we celebrate the Eucharist.

♫ We Come to Share God's Special Gift

We come to share God's
   special gift:
Jesus here in Eucharist
   for you, for me,
   for all God's family;
   for me, for you
God's love is always true!

We join with our parish for the celebration of Mass.

WE GATHER

✝ *Jesus, we celebrate your love for us.*

🏃 What are some school celebrations you enjoy? Act out ways you take part in one celebration.

WE BELIEVE

Every Sunday we gather as a parish to celebrate Mass. A priest leads us in this celebration.

We take part in the celebration of the Mass. We praise God by singing and praying. We listen to God's Word.

We offer our prayers to God. The priest does what Jesus did at the Last Supper.

We are sent out to share God's love with others.

WE RESPOND

 What can you do to take part in the celebration of Mass?

Three things you can do are hidden in the puzzle. Find and circle them.

```
P R A Y V W X Y
Z B X P S I N G
A L I S T E N J
```

At Mass this Sunday, do these things to praise God and remember his great love for us.

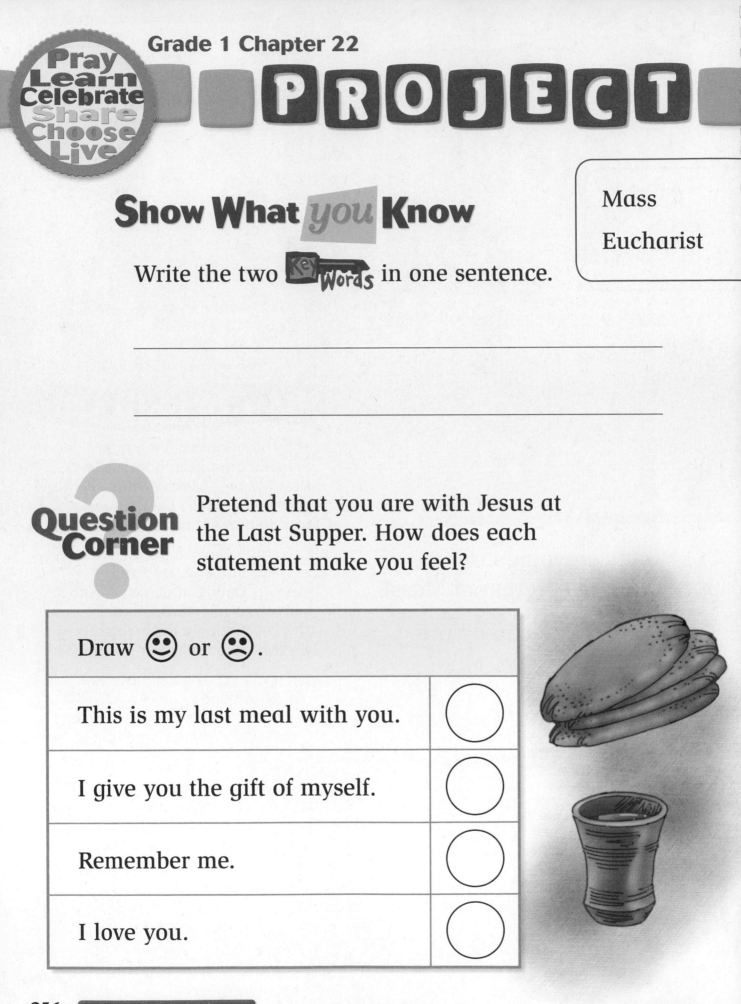

Pray Learn Celebrate Share Choose Live

PROJECT

Show What you Know

Write the two Key Words in one sentence.

Mass

Eucharist

_____

_____

Question Corner

Pretend that you are with Jesus at the Last Supper. How does each statement make you feel?

Draw 😊 or ☹️.	
This is my last meal with you.	◯
I give you the gift of myself.	◯
Remember me.	◯
I love you.	◯

D1SC1PLE

Pray
Learn
Celebrate
Share
Choose
Live

What's the Word?

Remember what Jesus said at the Last Supper.

"Take and eat; this is my body."
(Matthew 26:26)

"Drink from it, all of you, for this is my blood." (Matthew 26:27–28)

Thank Jesus for all he has done for us.

Reality Check

When is Jesus with you?

- ❏ When I am at Mass
- ❏ When I celebrate Jesus' life
- ❏ When I pray with my parish
- ❏ Always
- ❏ Another time: _____

_____

Take Home

The most important thing our parish does is celebrate Mass together on Sunday. People of the parish give their time to help us celebrate. Talk with your family about who is at Mass to help celebrate the Eucharist. Make a list together.

_____

_____

Use the words in the box to complete the sentences.

parish
Eucharist
Mass
meal
priest

1. The Last Supper is the special

_____ that Jesus

shared before he died.

2. The _____ is the

sacrament of the Body and Blood of

Jesus Christ.

3. The _____ is another name

for the celebration of the Eucharist.

4. A _____ leads us in the

celebration of the Mass.

5. We join with our _____ for

the celebration of Mass.

 In what ways is Jesus with us during
the celebration of Mass?

✝ We Gather in Prayer

Leader: Close your eyes and sit quietly. Think about all the gifts of God's creation. Now let us praise God for all these gifts.

🎵 Shout from the Mountains

Shout from the mountains,
Sing in the valleys,
Call from the waters,
Dance through the hills!
All of God's people,
All of God's creatures,
All of creation,
Join in the song!

And we sing:
Holy, holy, holy is God!
Holy, holy, holy and strong!

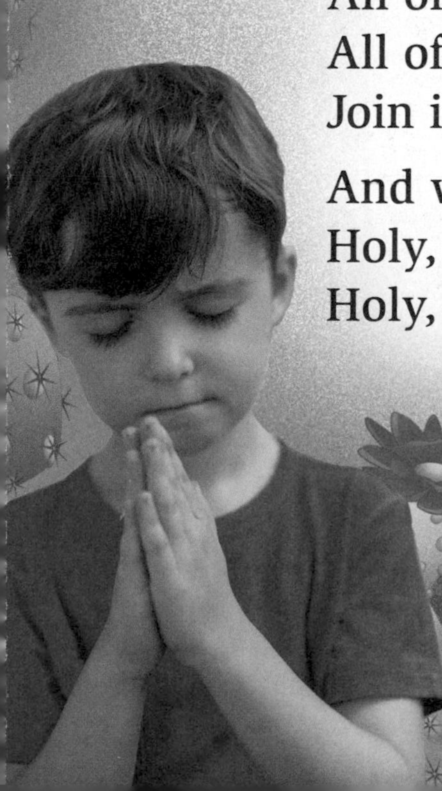

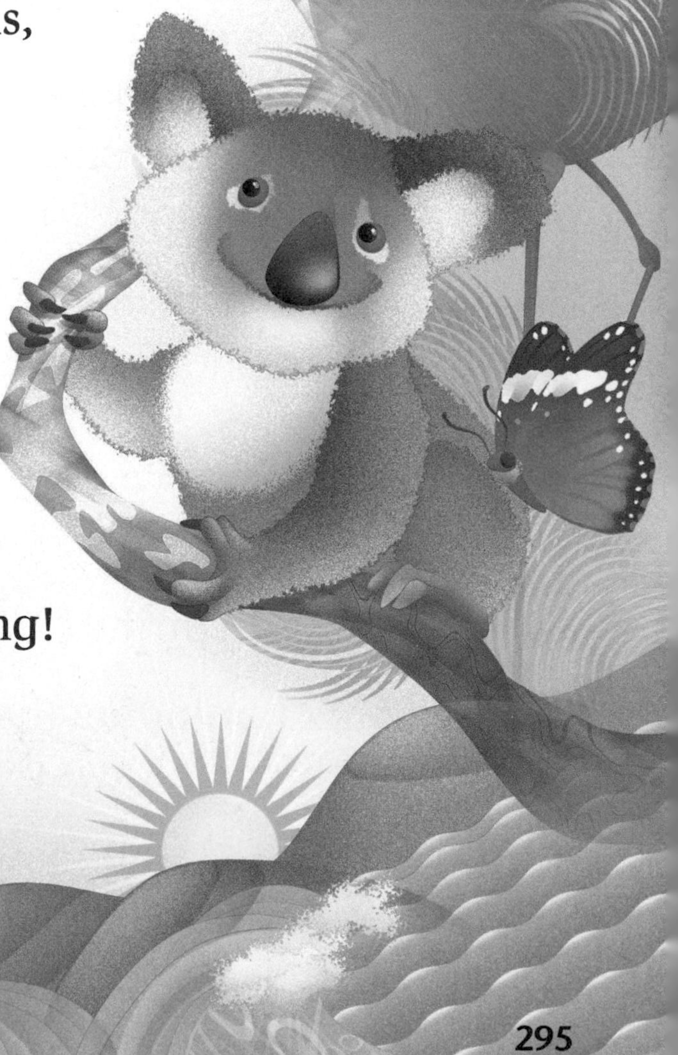

We gather to worship God.

WE GATHER

✟ *God, we worship you. We give you thanks.*

🧍 What are some ways we welcome people?
Act out some ways.

WE BELIEVE

The Mass is the Church's greatest celebration. The most important time that our parish comes together is for Sunday Mass.

As we gather, we welcome one another. We join together. We stand and sing. This shows we are happy to celebrate together.

The priest welcomes us. With the priest, we pray the Sign of the Cross. The priest says,
"The Lord be with you."

We answer together,
"And with your spirit."

These words remind us that Jesus is with us at Mass.

Then we ask God and one another for forgiveness.

We praise God by singing or praying aloud.
Our prayer begins:

"Glory to God

in the highest,
and on earth peace to people of good will."

Color the words that begin our
prayer of praise.

WE RESPOND

What are some ways the members of
your parish welcome one another as
the Mass begins?

Next Sunday, what
can you do to
take part in
the beginning
of Mass?

We listen to God's Word.

WE GATHER

✝ *God, we praise you for your glory.*

When do you listen to stories from the Bible? Write who or what your favorite story is about.

_____

_____

_____

WE BELIEVE

The Bible is the book of God's Word. At Sunday Mass we listen to three readings from the Bible. We listen carefully so that we may grow in God's love.

The first reading is about God's people who lived before Jesus Christ was born. The second reading is about the teachings of the Apostles. It is also about the beginning of the Church.

After each of these readings, the reader says, "The word of the Lord."

We answer, "Thanks be to God."

Next we stand and sing Alleluia or other words of praise. This shows we are ready to listen to the reading of the Gospel. The **Gospel** is the Good News about Jesus Christ and his teachings.

The priest or deacon reads the Gospel to us. Then he says,
"The Gospel of the Lord."

We answer,
"Praise to you, Lord Jesus Christ."

The priest or deacon talks to us about all the readings. We listen. We learn how we can grow as followers of Jesus. We learn how to be members of the Church.

After the priest's talk, we stand. We say aloud what we believe as Catholics.

Then we pray for the Church and all people. After each prayer, we say, "Lord, hear our prayer."

Key Word

Gospel the Good News about Jesus Christ and his teachings

WE RESPOND

At Mass next Sunday listen carefully to the readings. How can you show others you have heard God's Word?

As Catholics...

The word *Gospel* means the "Good News of Jesus Christ." The Good News is that Jesus is the Son of God, who told us of God the Father's love.

Jesus taught us how to live. He died and rose to new life for us. This is the Good News we celebrate.

What can you tell someone about the Good News of Jesus Christ?

Our gifts of bread and wine become the Body and Blood of Christ.

WE GATHER

✝ *God, we offer ourselves to you.*

Think about the ways your family gets ready for special meals. How do you get the table ready?

WE BELIEVE

The **altar** is the table of the Lord. The priest prepares the altar for the celebration of the Eucharist.

Everything we have is a gift from God. At the Eucharist we offer these gifts back to God. We offer ourselves, too.

People bring gifts of bread and wine to the priest. The priest prepares the gifts of bread and wine. We pray, "Blessed be God for ever."

Then we remember what Jesus said and did at the Last Supper. The priest takes the bread. He says,
"TAKE THIS, ALL OF YOU, AND EAT OF IT, FOR THIS IS MY BODY, WHICH WILL BE GIVEN UP FOR YOU."

Then the priest takes the cup of wine. He says,
"TAKE THIS, ALL OF YOU, AND DRINK FROM IT, FOR THIS IS THE CHALICE OF MY BLOOD . . ."

The bread and wine become the Body and Blood of Christ. This is done by the power of the Holy Spirit and through the words and actions of the priest. Jesus Christ is really present in the Eucharist.

We sing or pray, "Amen."
We are saying, "Yes, I believe."

WE RESPOND

Pray quietly. Thank Jesus for being with us in the Eucharist. Then together sing or say "Amen."

Key Word

altar the table of the Lord

We grow closer to Jesus and one another.

WE GATHER

✝ *Jesus, we believe you are present in the Eucharist.*

What is the prayer that Jesus taught us? When do you pray this prayer?

WE BELIEVE

After the bread and wine have become the Body and Blood of Christ, we get ready to receive Jesus. Together we pray or sing the Our Father.

Then we turn to the people who are near us. We share a sign of peace. We say a prayer to ask Jesus for forgiveness and peace.

Then the priest invites us to share in the Eucharist. The people who have received first Holy Communion come forward to receive the Body and Blood of Christ. They answer, "Amen."

While this is happening, we sing a song of thanks. This shows that we are joined with Jesus and all the members of the Church. We grow closer to him and one another.

Then there is some quiet time. We thank Jesus for giving himself to us in the Eucharist. After this the priest blesses us.
The priest or deacon may say, "Go in peace."
We say, "Thanks be to God."

We are sent to share with others the Good News of Jesus. We go out to live as Jesus' followers.

WE RESPOND

What are some ways you can grow closer to Jesus?

🎵 We Come to Share God's Special Gift

We come to share God's special gift:
Jesus here in Eucharist
For you, for me, for all God's family;
For me, for you God's love is always true!

PROJECT

Show What *you* Know

Guess the **Key Word** for each riddle.

Gospel

altar

> The priest prepares me for the celebration of the Eucharist. I am the table of the Lord.

I am the _____.

> To show you are ready to listen to me, you stand and sing words of praise. I am the Good News about Jesus Christ and his teachings.

I am the _____.

Pray Today

The prayers that the children are saying are from Sunday Mass.

Now, pass it on!

Lord, hear our prayer.

Thanks be to God.

DISCIPLE

Pray
Learn
Celebrate
Share
Choose
Live

What Would *you* do?

Imagine your friend asks you,
"What is the Good News about Jesus Christ?"

_____

_____

_____

What would you say to
him or her? Write it in
the speech bubble.

Do your best to participate
at Mass this Sunday!

Take Home

After Mass priests, deacons,
or extraordinary ministers
of Holy Communion take
the Eucharist to people who
cannot attend Mass because
they are sick. As a family, pray
for all those who are sick.

269

Circle the correct answer.

1. The altar is the _____ of the Lord.

   table   home

2. The _____ is the Good News about Jesus Christ and his teachings.

   Gospel   first reading

3. When we pray "Amen," we are saying, _____.

   "Yes, I believe"   "Forgive me"

4. When people receive the Body and Blood of Christ, they say _____.

   "Thank you"   "Amen"

5. We get ready to receive Jesus in Holy Communion by praying the _____.

   Our Father   Hail Mary

 What are some things we do at the beginning of Mass?

We Share God's Love

24

✝ We Gather in Prayer

Leader: After Jesus rose to new life, he visited his followers. Let us listen to Jesus' words when he first visited them.

📖 John 20:19, 21

Reader: Jesus came and stood near them. He said, "Peace be with you."

(John 20:21)

All: Jesus, you gave us your gifts of peace and love.

Leader: Jesus told his followers that he wanted them to share God's love with everyone. We are followers of Jesus. He wants us to share God's love, too.

All: Jesus, help us to share your gifts of love and peace with everyone.

Jesus shows us how to love and serve.

WE GATHER

✝ *Jesus, help us to follow you each day.*

Think of a time someone trusted you to do something important.
How did you feel after you did what they asked?

WE BELIEVE

Jesus trusted God his Father. He did the things his Father asked him to do. Jesus told everyone about God. He shared God's love with all people.

Jesus told his followers, "As I have loved you, so you also should love one another." (John 13:34) Jesus showed us how to love and serve God and one another, too.

We love and serve God by learning the ways he wants us to live. We try to do the things he wants us to do. We tell others about God and share his great love.

272

Look at the picture. Tell how the people are loving and serving God.

WE RESPOND

What is one thing you will do to share God's love today?

When we pray, we show God that we love him.

WE GATHER

✝ *God, we want to be close to you.*

When do you talk to members of your family?
When do you talk to your friends?
What do you talk about?

WE BELIEVE

We spend a lot of time with the people we love. We talk and listen to them. We share what is important to us. We grow closer to each other.

We show God we love him when we pray. Prayer is listening to and talking to God. We grow closer to God when we pray.

Jesus taught us that God is his Father. He prayed to his Father often. He wants us to pray often, too. We pray to the Blessed Trinity: God the Father, God the Son, and God the Holy Spirit.

We can pray by ourselves. We can pray with our families, with our friends, and with our parish. We can use our own words to pray. We can pray the prayers of the Church.

As Catholics...

There are many ways to pray. We can praise God. We can tell God we are sorry for something we have done wrong. We can thank God for his loving care. We can ask God for what we need. We can pray for other people.

Try to pray in one or more of these ways today.

WE RESPOND

Write a prayer that you will pray this week.

____

____

____

____

We share God's love with our families.

WE GATHER

✝ *Thank you, God, for our families.*

What do members of your family share with one another?

WE BELIEVE

God wants us to love and serve him. We do this when we share God's love with our families.

We share God's love with our families in these ways.

- We are kind and helpful.
- We obey our parents and all those who care for us.
- We take care of the things that belong to our family.
- We show our love for all family members.
- We say we are sorry and forgive one another.

Look at the pictures. Act out what the family members are doing. Tell what they may be saying to each other. Talk about the ways each family is sharing God's love.

WE RESPOND

Think about the ways your family shares God's love.

How can you thank your family for sharing God's love?

We share God's love with others.

WE GATHER

✞ *Holy Spirit, help us to live as Jesus did.*

Have you helped someone this week? How did you help?

WE BELIEVE

God made each of us. He made us to share God's love with everyone. We can join with our own families to share God's love. We can join with members of our parish to do this, too.

Look at the pictures on these pages. Talk about what is happening in each picture. Tell how the people are loving and serving God.

WE RESPOND

Name one way you will help your family and parish serve others this week.

_____

_____

_____

🎵 **Walk in Love**

Walk in love as Jesus loved,
let us walk in Jesus,
light up the world,
light up the world
with God's own love.

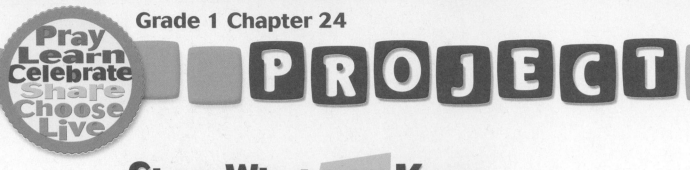

PROJECT

Show What *you* Know

There is an important word missing from these statements. Write it in.

Jesus shows us how to _____ and serve.

When we pray, we show God that we _____ him.

We share God's _____ with our families.

We share God's _____ with others.

Make *it* Happen

Parish priests lead us in the celebration of the Eucharist. They help us prepare to celebrate the other sacraments. They visit people who are sick. They help people learn more about the Bible and the Church. As a class, write a card to your parish priest to thank him for serving God and others.

DISCIPLE

Picture This

Draw a picture of:

a way that you show your family members you love them	a way that you show God you love him

↳ **DISCIPLE CHALLENGE** How are these ways alike? How are they different?

Take Home

Invite each member of your family to complete the following. Write your initials beside one thing you will do to share God's love with your family this week.

- I will be kind and helpful.
- I will obey my parents.
- I will take care of things that belong to my family.
- I will forgive others.

Circle the correct answer.

1. Do we serve God when we show others his love?

Yes   No

2. Do we share God's love with our family members when we take things that belong to them?

Yes   No

3. Do we share God's love when we forgive one another?

Yes   No

4. Did Jesus tell everyone about God?

Yes   No

5. Is there only one way to pray?

Yes   No

 How do we share God's love with our families?

We Honor Mary and the Saints

✝ We Gather in Prayer

Leader: God chose Mary to be the Mother of his own Son, Jesus.
Listen to God's Word.

📖 Luke 1:26–28, 35

Read Along

Before Jesus was born, God sent an angel to Mary. The angel said to Mary, "Hail, favored one! The Lord is with you." (Luke 1:28)
The angel told Mary that she was going to have a son. The angel told her, "The child to be born will be called holy, the Son of God." (Luke 1:35)

Leader: Joseph was Mary's husband. He loved and cared for Mary and Jesus.

🎵 Joseph Was a Good Man

Joseph was a good man,
a good man, a good man,
Joseph was a good man,
chosen by the Lord.
And Joseph loved a lady,
Joseph loved a lady,
Joseph loved a lady,
chosen by the Lord.

283

Mary is the mother of Jesus.

WE GATHER

✝ *God, you give us people who care for us.*

How do mothers care for and help their children? Act out some ways.

WE BELIEVE

God asked Mary to be the Mother of his Son. Mary said "yes" to God. Mary gave birth to God's only Son, Jesus.

Mary loved Jesus. Mary cared for him. She helped him learn many things.

All through his life, Mary saw the wonderful things that Jesus did. Mary listened to Jesus teach. She watched him heal the sick. She celebrated special times with him.

Jesus always loved his mother. He wanted his followers to love and care for her, too. Mary shows us how to live as Jesus asks us to.

WE RESPOND

Jesus wants us to love his mother. How can we show our love for Mary?

The Church honors Mary.

WE GATHER

✝ *Holy Mary, pray for us.*

When we honor people, we show them how special they are to us.

Name someone you would like to honor. Tell why.

WE BELIEVE

The Church honors Mary. We honor her because she is the mother of Jesus. To show our love for Mary, we sometimes call her "Our Lady" and "The Blessed Mother."

Unscramble the words to complete the sentence.

R M O E T H   U R C H C H

We also honor Mary as the

__M__ ___ ___ ___ ___ ___ of the __C__ ___ ___ ___ ___ ___ .

We honor Mary in different ways. One way is to celebrate her feast days. On these days, we remember special times in the lives of Mary and Jesus.

The Church also has prayers to honor Mary. We can say these prayers often. One special prayer that we say is the Hail Mary.

Hail Mary, full of grace,
the Lord is with you!
Blessed are you among women,
and blessed is the fruit of
    your womb, Jesus.
Holy Mary, Mother of God,
pray for us sinners,
now and at the hour of our death.
Amen.

WE RESPOND

Talk with a friend about ways you can honor Mary this week. Then choose one you will do.

Pray together the Hail Mary.

As Catholics...

We honor Mary in a special way on certain days of the year. On some of these days, parishes gather together for processions. On these special prayer walks, the people sing songs to Mary and pray special prayers. They put flowers in front of a statue of Mary. In this way they honor Mary.

Find out ways your parish honors Mary.

The saints are close to God.

✝ *God, keep us close to you.*

When you listen to stories about your family, how do you feel? What are some things you learn?

The Church shares stories about many of Jesus' followers. Some of these stories are about the saints.

The **saints** are followers of Jesus who have died and now live forever with God.

The saints tried to live the way Jesus asked. They loved God very much. They tried to share God's love with others. They prayed to God often.

Saint Katharine Drexel began schools for Native American and African American children.

Saint Francis Xavier taught the people of India to know God.

Saint Andrew Kim Taegon was the first priest and pastor in Korea.

Look at the pictures on these pages.
They show some saints of the Church.
Read the sentence below each picture.

Use a yellow crayon.
Highlight each saint's name.

Talk about some people you know who do the things these saints did.

WE RESPOND

Which of these saints can you be like?

Key Word

saints followers of Jesus who have died and now live forever with God

Saint Anne was the mother of Mary and the grandmother of Jesus.

Saint Teresa of Avila wrote books and letters to help people love Jesus.

Saint John Vianney was a parish priest who served his people.

We honor all the saints of the Church.

WE GATHER

✝ *Holy Spirit, help us to become saints.*

Look at the picture. The children
are dressed as their favorite saints.
Who is your favorite saint? Tell why.

WE BELIEVE

There are many, many saints.
We do not know all their names.

All the saints loved God very much.
They put God first in their lives.
They tried to be kind and fair.
They shared God's peace with others.

Saint John Bosco

Saint Mary Magdalen

Saint Peter

Saint Elizabeth Seton

The Church has a special day to honor all the saints. We call this day the Feast of All Saints. This day is November 1.

On this day we gather with our parish family. We celebrate Mass. At Mass we thank God for all the saints.

All through the year, we can ask the saints to pray for us. We can ask them to help us grow close to God. We can honor them by trying to be more like them.

WE RESPOND

Tell some ways we can be like the saints. Ask the saints to pray for us.

♫ When the Saints Go Marching In

Oh, when the saints
  go marching in,
Oh, when the saints
  go marching in,
O Lord, I want to be in that number,
When the saints go marching in.

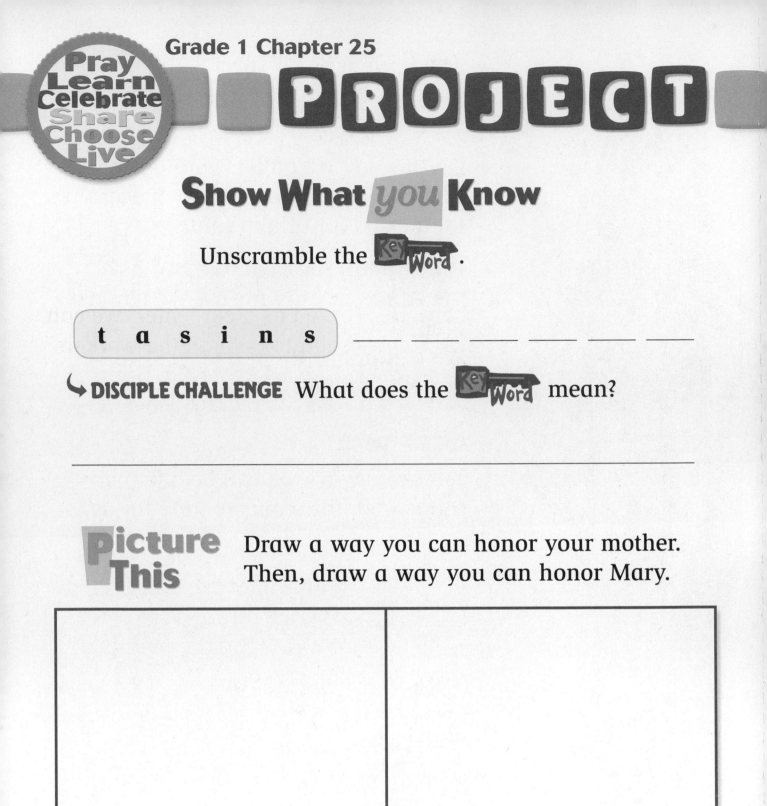

PROJECT

Pray Learn Celebrate Share Choose Live

Show What you Know

Unscramble the Key Word.

t a s i n s _____

↳ **DISCIPLE CHALLENGE** What does the Key Word mean?

_____

Picture This Draw a way you can honor your mother.
Then, draw a way you can honor Mary.

How are these ways alike? How are they different?

DISCIPLE

Saint Stories

Saint Joseph was the husband of Mary and foster father of Jesus. He cared for them. He worked as a carpenter. We can ask Saint Joseph to help all the workers of the world. We celebrate the Feast of Saint Joseph the Worker on May 1.

Make *it* Happen

Jesus wants us to love his mother Mary. We can show our love by praying to her. Decorate the first words of this prayer.

More *to* Explore

Many people are named after a saint. Are you? Learn about this saint or another saint that interests you. Visit the library or *Lives of the Saints* at **www.webelieveweb.com**.

Take Home

Family was very important to Jesus. He and Mary and Joseph loved and cared for one another. Who loves and cares for you? Make a family tree. Include your family members. Talk about your family tree.

Circle the correct answer.

1. Mary is the _____ of Jesus.

mother   sister

2. A special prayer we honor Mary with is the _____.

Our Father   Hail Mary

3. _____ are followers of Jesus who have died and now live forever with God.

Saints   Sacraments

4. There are _____ saints.

many   just a few

5. The saints are _____ God.

far away from   close to

 What are some of the things we do to honor Mary?

We Care for the Gifts of God's Creation

✝ **We Gather in Prayer**

Leader: Close your eyes and sit quietly. Think about all the gifts of God's creation. Now let us praise God for all these gifts.

🎵 **Shout from the Mountains**

Shout from the mountains,
Sing in the valleys,
Call from the waters,
Dance through the hills!
All of God's people,
All of God's creatures,
All of creation,
Join in the song!

And we sing:
Holy, holy, holy is God!
Holy, holy, holy and strong!

The world is God's gift to us.

✝ *Thank you, God, for all you have made.*

Close your eyes and picture yourself in your favorite outdoor place. Tell where you are. Tell what you see.

WE BELIEVE

God has given us all of creation to use and enjoy. The world is God's gift to us. It is full of beautiful places and wonderful plants and animals.

God asks us to take care of his creation. The gifts of creation are for all people. God wants people everywhere to be able to use these gifts. God wants us to share these gifts of creation.

Look at the pictures on these pages. Tell how the people are taking care of God's creation.

What are some ways you can share the gifts of God's creation?

Draw a picture to finish this prayer.

God, we want to take care of the world. Help us to

Animals are part of God's creation.

WE GATHER

✝ *God, help us share the gifts of your creation.*

Look at the animals on this page. Where can you find these animals?

WE BELIEVE

God created the world and filled it with animals. Animals are wonderful gifts from God.

Read Along

"Then God said, 'Let the earth bring forth all kinds of living creatures: cattle, creeping things, and wild animals of all kinds.' And so it happened: God made all kinds of wild animals, all kinds of cattle, and all kinds of creeping things of the earth. God saw how good it was." (Genesis 1:24–25)

When God created people, he told them to watch over the animals.

We care for the animals when we make sure they have food to eat and water to drink. We also make sure they have a place to live. We try to learn more about them and what they need.

WE RESPOND

What animals can you take care of?

 Who are some people in your town who take care of animals? Write or draw about what these people do.

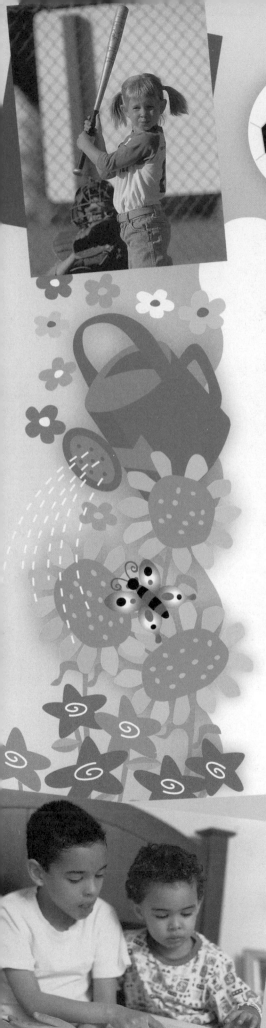

We are all important to God.

WE GATHER

✝ *We praise you, God.*

Find a partner. Tell some ways you two are alike. Name some ways you are different.

WE BELIEVE

God created each one of us. No two people in the world are exactly alike. We enjoy different things. We have different gifts and talents. We look different from one another.

God wants us to use our gifts and talents. We can use them to take care of creation and to care for one another.

What are your special gifts? How can you share them with others?

Let us thank God for making all people.

🎵 **Malo! Malo! Thanks Be to God**

(Sing each line two times)

Malo! Malo!
Thanks be to God!
O-bri-ga-do!
Alleluia!
Gra-ci-as!
Kam-sa-ham-ni-da!
Malo! Malo!
Thanks be to God!

As Catholics...

Each of us is special. God loves each and every one of us. He gave us the gift of life. We can show God our thanks for the gift of life. One way we can do this is by taking care of ourselves.

We can take care of ourselves by:
- eating the right foods
- getting enough sleep
- keeping ourselves clean
- obeying rules.

What other ways can we thank God for the gift of life?

301

We care for and respect all people.

WE GATHER

✝ *Holy, holy, holy is God!*

Think about your:

- parents and grandparents
- brothers, sisters, or cousins
- neighbors
- classmates.

How do you talk to one another? How do you act toward one another?

WE BELIEVE

Jesus often talked about ways we should treat other people. This is what he told his followers one day.

Read Along

"Do to others whatever you would have them do to you." (Matthew 7:12)

Jesus meant that we should treat other people the way we want to be treated. We should show kindness and respect. We should share God's love with all people.

Here are some ways we can do this.

- Be polite. Say polite things like "Please" and "Thank you."

- Respect other people's belongings. Do not take anything without asking.

- Tell the truth. Do not tell lies.

- Ask for forgiveness if we have done something wrong. Say "I'm sorry."

- Forgive other people when they tell us they are sorry.

Work with a partner. Choose one of the ideas above. Make up a play that shows people doing this. Then act it out.

WE RESPOND

Who can you show kindness and respect for this week?

PROJECT

Show What *you* Know

Describe God's creation.
Use words or pictures.

Reality Check

Today I can share God's love by

❏ being polite.

❏ telling lies.

❏ taking others' belongings
without asking.

❏ asking for forgiveness.

❏ forgiving others.

Pray
Learn
Celebrate
Share
Choose
Live

Question Corner

Every person is special to God. You are special to God. Share your story. Draw a picture of yourself. Answer the questions below.

What makes you a disciple of Jesus?

_____

What is a special gift you have from God?

_____

How can you help take care of God's creation?

_____

Take Home

Talk together about ways you can help care for God's creation as a family.

CHAPTER TEST

Use the words in the box to complete the sentences.

respect

treat

created

gift

animals

1. The world is God's

_____ to all people.

2. God told people to watch over the

_____ he created.

3. All people in the world are

_____ by God.

4. Jesus told us to _____ others
the way we want to be treated.

5. Jesus wants us to treat all people with kindness

and _____.

TALK ABOUT IT How can we share God's love with
other people?

"This is the day the LORD has made;
let us rejoice in it and be glad."

Psalm 118:24

SEASONAL

CHAPTER 27

This chapter celebrates the entire
Easter season.

The Church celebrates that Jesus rose to new life.

WE GATHER

What are some signs of new life? Share your ideas with one another.

WE BELIEVE

Easter is a time of great joy. The Three Days lead us to Easter Sunday. It is time to rejoice!

During Mass on Easter Sunday, we listen to the story of Jesus' rising from the dead. Here is what Saint Matthew tells us.

📖 Matthew 28:1–10

Narrator: "After the sabbath, as the first day of the week was dawning, Mary Magdalene and the other Mary came to see the tomb. And behold, there was a great earthquake; for an angel of the Lord descended from heaven, approached, rolled back the stone, and sat upon it." (Matthew 28:1–2)

Reader: The angel was dressed in clothes as white as snow. It was so bright.

Reader: The angel had come so quickly. The guards were very scared.

Reader: The angel told the women not to be afraid. Jesus has risen from the dead.

Reader: The angel told them to go and tell the other followers that they would see Jesus soon.

Reader: The women went to find the others. On their way, Jesus met them. The women went to Jesus. They bowed before him.

Narrator: Then Jesus said to them, "Do not be afraid. Go tell my brothers to go to Galilee, and there they will see me."

(Matthew 28:10)

During Easter we celebrate that Jesus rose to new life.

Decorate the Alleluia banner with signs of new life.

Alleluia!

✝ We Respond in Prayer

Leader: Praised be the risen Jesus.

All: Let us rejoice and be glad, alleluia!

🎵 **Alleluia No. 1**

Chorus
> Alleluia, alleluia!
> Give thanks to the risen
>   Lord.
> Alleluia, alleluia!
> Give praise to his name.

> Spread the good news o'er
>   all the earth:
> Jesus has died and has risen. (Chorus)

PROJECT DISCIPLE

Pray Learn Celebrate Share Choose Live

Celebrate!

Use the code to discover an important message.

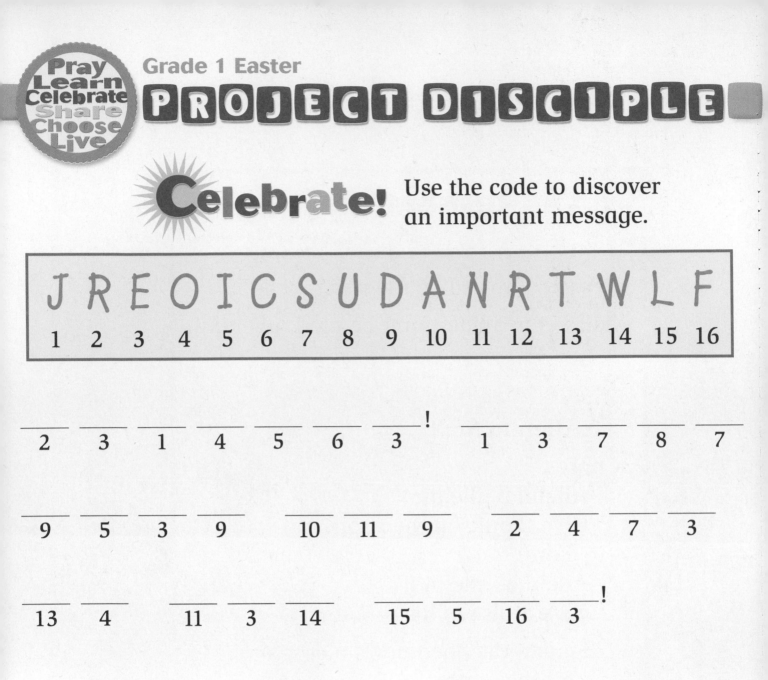

J	R	E	O	I	C	S	U	D	A	N	R	T	W	L	F
1	2	3	4	5	6	7	8	9	10	11	12	13	14	15	16

___ ___ ___ ___ ___ ___ ___ ! ___ ___ ___ ___ ___
2   3   1   4   5   6   3   1   3   7   8   7

___ ___ ___ ___   ___ ___ ___   ___ ___ ___ ___
9   5   3   9   10 11   9   2   4   7   3

___ ___   ___ ___ ___   ___ ___ ___ ___ !
13 4   11   3 14   15   5 16   3

Fast Facts

Eggs are a symbol of new life. So eggs are a symbol of Easter too! At Easter Jesus rose to new life.

Take Home

With your family list ways that you celebrate Easter together.

UNIT TEST

Circle the correct answer.

1. Is the Eucharist the sacrament of
the Body and Blood of Jesus Christ?   **Yes   No**

2. Does Jesus want us to treat people
unfairly?   **Yes   No**

3. Do we call the celebration of the
Eucharist the Mass?   **Yes   No**

4. Did the saints put God last in their lives?   **Yes   No**

5. Does the Church honor Mary in
different ways?   **Yes   No**

Write the correct word to finish each sentence.

6. The _____ is the
Church's greatest celebration.

7. The _____ are
followers of Jesus who have died and now
live forever with God.

8. The _____ is the table
of the Lord.

altar

saints

Mass

continued on next page   **313**

9. Choose and circle one of the pictures. Write how the people are sharing God's love.

_____

10. Write sentences to tell a few ways you can share God's love.

_____

_____

_____

_____

_____

The Saints and Prayer

Part 1   I Open My Heart

What have you learned about saints? Think of one saint you have learned about. Complete the stained glass window to show this saint.

Share your stained glass saint picture. Share what you know about this saint with the group.

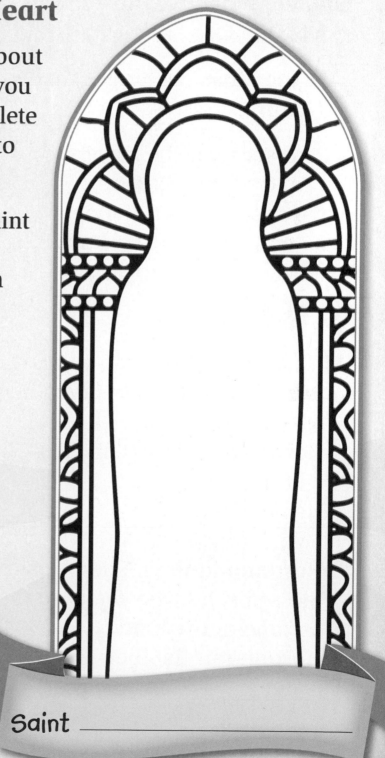

Saint _____

The Saints and Prayer

Part 2 We Come Together for Prayer

Leader: When we pray at Mass, we worship God.

In the Mass, we praise God with the saints. The priest prays:

And so, with the Angels
  and all the Saints,
we declare your glory,
as with one voice we acclaim:
(Based on Eucharistic Prayer II)

We respond:

All: (*All raise arms up, palms facing upward, as a sign of praise.*)
Holy, Holy, Holy Lord God
  of hosts.
Heaven and earth are full of
  your glory.
Hosanna in the highest.
Blessed is he who comes in the
  name of the Lord.
Hosanna in the highest.
Amen.

The Saints and Prayer

Part 3 I Cherish God's Word

"Be imitators of God, as beloved children, and live in love, as Christ loved us." (Ephesians 5:1–2)

LISTEN to the reading from Scripture. Pay close attention to the reading.

REFLECT on what you heard. Think about:

- How the saints loved others, as Christ did.

- How can you follow the example of the saints?

SHARE your thoughts and feelings with God in prayer. Speak to God as a friend.

CONTEMPLATE or sit quietly and think about God's Word in the Scripture passage from the Letter of Saint Paul to the Ephesians above.

Communion of Saints tapestries, by John Nava, Cathedral of Our Lady of the Angels, Los Angeles, CA

Catholic
Identity
Retreat

The Saints and Prayer

Part 4   I Value My Catholic Faith

Saints loved others as Christ did. The best way
to honor a saint is to follow his or her example.
Write what you think a saint would do.

What's happening?	What would a saint do?
There is a new student in your class.	_____ _____
Someone is being bullied in the playground.	_____ _____
A younger child gets hurt coming to school.	_____ _____

The Saints and Prayer

Part 5 I Celebrate Catholic Identity

Pope Francis said, "To see God, to be like God: this is our hope."

(Pope Francis, homily for Solemnity of All Saints, November 1, 2013)

The saints give us hope. We can follow their example.

You can be a saint! Work with a partner to list the things you could do in your life to follow the example of the saints. Tell about good things you have done, like the saints.

Share your list with the whole group.

Catholic
Identity
Retreat

The Saints and Prayer

Part 6   I Honor My Catholic Identity

Leader: Mary, the mother of Jesus, and all the other saints help us by their prayers. They pray for us that we may live forever with God as they do. Listen to God's Word.

Reader: "May the God of peace . . . make you perfectly holy."
(1 Thessalonians 5:23)

Leader: God, we praise you for the lives of the saints. Hear their prayers for us and help us to learn from their example. Bow your heads for a blessing.

May God, the glory and joy of
   the Saints,
who has caused you to be strengthened
by means of their outstanding prayers,
bless you with unending blessings.

All: Amen.

(Solemn Blessing, Solemnity of All Saints)

Catholic Identity Retreat

Bringing the Retreat Home

The Saints and Prayer

Retreat Recap

Review the pages of your child's *Celebrating Catholic Identity: Prayer* retreat. Ask your child to tell you about the retreat. Talk about the saints and prayer:

- Saints are followers of Jesus who loved him very much.
- We honor the saints throughout the year and are united with the saints when we pray at Mass.
- The saints pray for us.

Patron Saint of the Family

"Dedicate" your family to a patron saint. Together choose a saint that has particular meaning for your family. Compose a family prayer in honor of this saint. You may wish to display an image of this saint in the home.

Saint _____

Take a Moment

Many prayers by or in honor of the saints have become an important part of our Catholic tradition. Think of one of these prayers that you know, and pray it aloud together. For example, the Hail Mary honors our greatest saint, Mary, the Mother of God. You may wish to review the *Prayers and Practices* or *Catholic Identity Home Companion* at the end of your child's book for further ideas.

Family Prayer

A litany is a prayer made up of short titles for God, Jesus, Mary, or other saints or holy people. After each title, we pray a short response, such as "Hear our prayer" or "Pray for us." Pray together a litany using the names of saints. You may wish to review your child's Chapter 25 for saints to include.

For more resources, see the *Catholic Identity Home Companion* at the end of this book.

Why We Believe
As a Catholic Family

What if someone asks us:

- Why do Catholics have devotions to saints?

The following resources can help us to respond:

Devotions are expressions of prayer that are handed down through the centuries. Many devotions honor Mary, and other devotions honor a particular saint or group of saints. Saints are our fellow Christians who are now with God in Heaven and whose holy lives have taught us the way of discipleship.

When we pray to the saints, we are really asking the saints to pray to God for us—to *intercede* for us. The practice of asking the saints for help in living the Christian life dates to the earliest days of the Church.

🌱 What does Scripture say?

"*We are surrounded by so great a cloud of witnesses. . . .*"; "*. . . the assembly of the firstborn enrolled in heaven, and God the judge of all, and the spirits of the just made perfect.*" (Hebrews 12:1, 23)

"*I kneel before the Father, from whom every family in heaven and on earth is named.*" (Ephesians 3:14–15)

All grace and power come from God. But God grants special gifts to the saints to help us as we are still journeying to Heaven. We ask for their blessing; we ask them to join with us in our prayer before God. As Catholics we can be in relationship with saints, with all in Heaven. It is a beautiful element of Catholic faith that we should celebrate. It is called the Communion of Saints.

Perhaps you have encountered questions about our practice of asking the saints to pray for us. Millions of Christians have lived before us, and because of their holy lives, the Church honors them and calls them saints. Any person in Heaven is a saint. Over the history of Christianity, the Church has given the official title of "Saint" to people known to have led particularly remarkable lives of holiness and who have had verifiable miracles occur through their intercession.

🌱 What does the Church say?

"*By keeping the memorials of the saints—first of all the holy Mother of God, then the apostles, the martyrs, and other saints—on fixed days of the liturgical year, the Church on earth shows that she is united with the liturgy of heaven. She gives glory to Christ for having accomplished his salvation in his glorified members; their example encourages her on her way to the Father.*" (CCC, 1195)

"*What is the Church if not the assembly of all the saints?*" (Saint Nicetas, one of the Church Fathers, A.D. 334–414, as quoted in CCC, 946)

"*Do not weep, for I shall be more useful to you after my death, and I shall help you then more effectively than during my life.*" (Saint Dominic, founder of the Dominicans, about 1170–1221, as quoted in CCC, 956)

Notes:

CONGRATULATIONS ON COMPLETING YOUR YEAR AS A GRADE 1 DISCIPLE!

Fold on this line.

PROJECT DISCIPLE LOG

Pray
Learn
Celebrate
Share
Choose
Live

A RECORD OF MY JOURNEY AS A GRADE 1 DISCIPLE

_____
Name

✂ Cut on this line.

Disciples of Jesus listen to and share God's Word.

My picture of my favorite story about Jesus

Disciples of Jesus pray every day.

A prayer I learned this year is

_____.

I pray this prayer

❏ by myself

❏ with my family

❏ with my classmates

❏ with my parish.

My prayer for summer is

_____.

Disciples of Jesus learn about their faith.

One thing I learned this year

- about following Jesus is

_____.

- about sharing my faith with others is

_____.

✂ Cut on this line.

Disciples of Jesus make loving choices.

This year I made a loving choice

- to care for God's world by

_____.

- to help my family by

_____.

This summer, I can show love for others by

_____.

Disciples of Jesus live out their faith.

This summer I will live out my faith when I am

- ❏ with my family
- ❏ with my friends
- ❏ on vacation
- ❏ on day trips
- ❏ in my neighborhood
- ❏ in church

❏ _____.

Disciples of Jesus celebrate the Church year.

My favorite time of the Church year was

_____.

I celebrated with

_____.

We celebrated by

_____.

End-of-Year Prayer Service

✝ We Gather in Prayer

Leader: We have learned many things about God this year.

Group 1: God is our loving Father.

Group 2: God sent his own Son, Jesus, to us.

Group 3: God shares his life and love with us.

Group 4: God wants us to share his love with others.

Leader: God, we want to remember all of these good things.

All: God, thank you for all your wonderful gifts. We believe that you are with us always. We want to share your love with others this summer.

🎵 We Celebrate With Joy

We celebrate with joy and gladness
We celebrate God's love for us.
We celebrate with joy and gladness
God with us today.
God with us today.

Find these things in your parish church:

1. sanctuary
2. altar
3. crucifix
4. tabernacle
5. sanctuary lamp
6. ambo (pulpit)
7. chalice
8. paten
9. cruets
10. presider's chair
11. processional cross
12. baptismal font or pool
13. Stations of the Cross
14. Reconciliation room or confessional

You are learning and living out ways to be a disciple of Jesus Christ.

Look what awaits you in:

We∙Believe Grade 2: Jesus Shares God's Life.

You will learn about and live out that

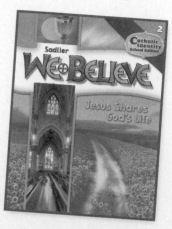

- Jesus Christ is with us always.
- Jesus calls us to Penance and Reconciliation.
- Jesus gives himself in the Eucharist.
- We live our Catholic faith.

Until next year, pay attention each time you go to Mass. Look around you. Listen.

Here is one thing I know about the ways Jesus shares God's life with us.

_____

Here is one thing that I want to learn more about next year.

_____

We are blessed to share in God's life!

My Mass Book

Fold on this line.

Cut on this line.

The priest blesses us. The priest or deacon may say, "Go in peace."
We say,

"Thanks be to God."

We go out to live as Jesus' followers.

We welcome one another. We stand and sing. We pray the Sign of the Cross. The priest says, "The Lord be with you."
We answer,

"And with your spirit."

We gather with our parish. We remember and celebrate what Jesus said and did at the Last Supper.

Cut on this line.

Fold on this line.

We ask God and one another for forgiveness. We praise God as we sing,

"Glory to God in the highest, and on earth peace to people of good will."

Glory to God

Then the priest invites us to share in the Eucharist. As people receive the Body and Blood of Christ, they answer,

"Amen."

While this is happening, we sing a song of thanks.

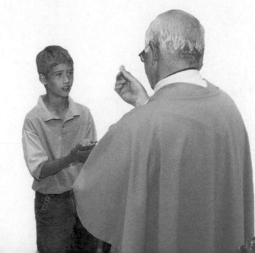

We get ready to receive Jesus. Together we pray or sing the Our Father. Then we share a sign of peace. We say,

"Peace be with you."

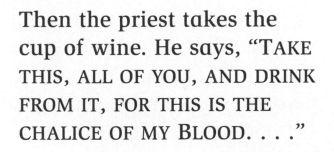

Cut on this line.

We listen to two readings from the Bible. After each one, the reader says, "The word of the Lord." We answer,

"Thanks be to God."

Then the priest takes the cup of wine. He says, "TAKE THIS, ALL OF YOU, AND DRINK FROM IT, FOR THIS IS THE CHALICE OF MY BLOOD. . . ."

We stand to say aloud what we believe as Catholics. Then we pray for the Church and all people. After each prayer we say,

"Lord, hear our prayer."

Fold on this line.

We stand and sing **Alleluia.**

The priest or deacon reads the Gospel. Then he says, "The Gospel of the Lord." We answer,

"Praise to you, Lord Jesus Christ."

Cut on this line.

Fold on this line.

We sing or pray,

"Amen."

We believe Jesus Christ is really present in the Eucharist.

The priest prepares the altar. People bring gifts of bread and wine to the priest. The priest prepares these gifts. We pray,

"Blessed be God for ever."

Then we remember what Jesus said and did at the Last Supper. The priest takes the bread. He says, "TAKE THIS, ALL OF YOU, AND EAT OF IT, FOR THIS IS MY BODY, WHICH WILL BE GIVEN UP FOR YOU."

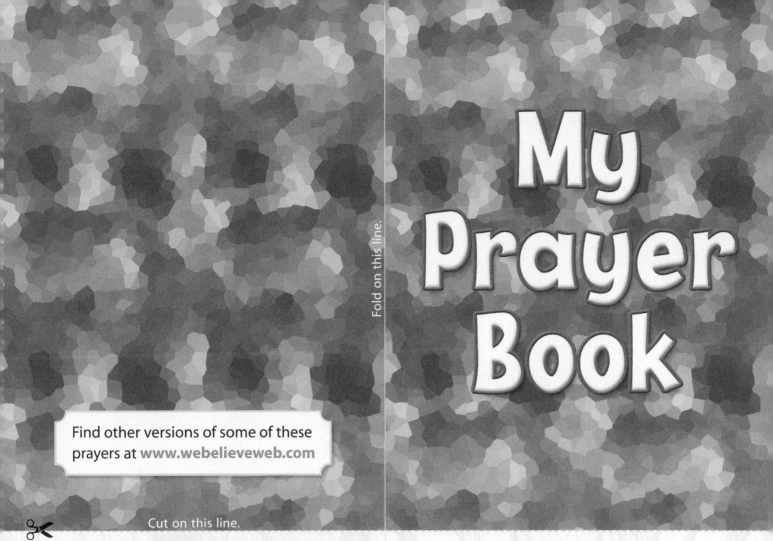

Fold on this line.

My Prayer Book

Find other versions of some of these prayers at **www.webelieveweb.com**

Cut on this line.

Angel of God

Angel of God,
my guardian dear,
to whom God's love commits
    me here,
ever this day be at my side,
to light and guard, to rule
    and guide.

Amen.

Glory Be to the Father

Glory be to the Father
and to the Son
and to the Holy Spirit
as it was in the beginning
is now, and ever shall be
world without end.

Amen.

Sign of the Cross

In the name of the Father,
and of the Son,
and of the Holy Spirit.

Amen.

Fold on this line.

Cut on this line.

Act of Contrition

Read Along

My God,
I am sorry for my sins with all my heart.
In choosing to do wrong
and failing to do good,
I have sinned against you
whom I should love above all things.
I firmly intend, with your help,
to do penance,
to sin no more,
and to avoid whatever leads me to sin.
Our Savior Jesus Christ
suffered and died for us.
In his name, my God, have mercy.

Our Father

Our Father, who art
  in heaven,
hallowed be thy name;
thy kingdom come;
thy will be done on earth
  as it is in heaven.

he ascended into heaven,
  and is seated at the right hand
  of God the Father almighty;
from there he will come to judge
  the living and the dead.

I believe in the Holy Spirit,
  the holy catholic Church,
  the communion of saints,
  the forgiveness of sins,
  the resurrection of the body,
  and life everlasting.

Amen.

The Apostles' Creed

Read Along

I believe in God the
  Father almighty,
  Creator of heaven and earth,

and in Jesus Christ,
  his only Son, our Lord,
  who was conceived by
  the Holy Spirit,
  born of the Virgin Mary,
  suffered under Pontius Pilate,
  was crucified, died and
  was buried;
  he descended into hell;
  on the third day he rose again
  from the dead;

Fold on this line.

Give us this day our
  daily bread;
and forgive us our
  trespasses
as we forgive those who
  trespass against us;
and lead us not into
  temptation,
but deliver us from evil.

Amen.

Grace Before Meals

Bless us, O Lord, and these
  your gifts
which we are about
  to receive
from your goodness.
Through Christ our Lord.

Amen.

Holy Mary, Mother of God,
pray for us sinners,
now and at the hour of
  our death.

Amen.

Hail Mary

Hail Mary, full of grace,
the Lord is with you!
Blessed are you among
   women,
and blessed is the fruit of
   your womb, Jesus.

Fold on this line.

Cut on this line.

Grace After Meals

We give you thanks
   almighty God
for these and all your gifts,
which we have received
   through
Christ our Lord.

Amen.

Morning Offering

My God, I offer you today
all that I think and do
   and say,
uniting it with what
   was done
on earth, by Jesus Christ,
your Son.

Evening Prayer

Dear God, before I sleep
I want to thank you for
   this day
so full of your kindness
and your joy.
I close my eyes to rest
safe in your loving care.

The Seven Sacraments

The Sacraments of Christian Initiation
> Baptism
>
> Confirmation
>
> Eucharist

The Sacraments of Healing
> Penance and Reconciliation
>
> Anointing of the Sick

The Sacraments at the Service of Communion
> Holy Orders
>
> Matrimony

The Ten Commandments

1. I am the LORD your God: you shall not have strange gods before me.

2. You shall not take the name of the LORD your God in vain.

3. Remember to keep holy the LORD'S Day.

4. Honor your father and your mother.

5. You shall not kill.

6. You shall not commit adultery.

7. You shall not steal.

8. You shall not bear false witness against your neighbor.

9. You shall not covet your neighbor's wife.

10. You shall not covet your neighbor's goods.

Glossary

altar (page 265)
the table of the Lord

Apostles (page 97)
the twelve men Jesus chose to
lead his followers

Baptism (page 196)
the sacrament in which we
become children of God and
members of the Church

Bible (page 21)
the book of God's Word

Blessed Trinity (page 36)
One God in the Three Persons:
God the Father, God the Son, and
God the Holy Spirit

Christmas (page 47)
the time when we celebrate the
birth of God's Son, Jesus

Church (page 133)
all the people who believe in Jesus
and follow his teachings

commandments (page 71)
laws or rules given to us
by God

creation (page 21)
everything God made

Easter Sunday (page 115)
the special day we celebrate
that Jesus Christ rose to
new life

Eucharist (page 250)
the sacrament of the Body
and Blood of Jesus Christ

Gospel (page 263)
the Good News about Jesus
Christ and his teachings

grace (page 199)
God's life in us

Holy Family (page 48)
the family of Jesus, Mary,
and Joseph

Lord's Prayer (page 101)
the prayer Jesus taught his
followers

Mass (page 252)
another name for the celebration
of the Eucharist

parish (page 173)
a group of Catholics who join
together to share God's love

pastor (page 176)
the priest who is the leader of
the parish

peacemaker (page 213)
a person who works for peace

Penance and Reconciliation
(page 225) the sacrament in which
we receive and celebrate God's
forgiveness

Pentecost (page 125)
the day the Holy Spirit came to
Jesus' followers

prayer (page 39)
listening to and talking to God

sacrament (page 189)
a special sign given to us by Jesus

saints (page 289)
followers of Jesus who have died
and now live forever with God

Sign of the Cross (page 39)
a prayer to the Blessed Trinity

Temple (page 113)
the holy place in Jerusalem where
the Jewish People prayed

trust (page 61)
to believe in someone's love for us

worship (page 175)
to give God thanks and praise

Index

The following is a list of topics that appear in the pupil's text.
Boldface indicates an entire chapter.

Catholic Identity Q&A

In this section, you will find questions and answers that review the content in your *We Believe: Catholic Identity Edition* book this year. Each question in this section covers the key Catholic teachings in your book, in chapter order. Answer each question to review what you have learned—whether you use this section at home, in school, or in the parish. The answers provided will strengthen your understanding of your Catholic faith and help to reinforce your Catholic Identity.

The *CCC* references after each answer indicate where to find further information about that answer in the *Catechism of the Catholic Church*.

Q: Why did God create us?

A: God created us to know, love, and serve him.
CCC, 356, 357, 358

Q: What is the Blessed Trinity?

A: The Blessed Trinity is One God in Three Persons: God the Father, God the Son, and God the Holy Spirit. *CCC*, 254

Q: What is prayer?

A: Prayer is listening to and talking to God. *CCC*, 2559

CCC = Catechism of the Catholic Church

Q: What is the Holy Family?

A: The Holy Family is Jesus, Mary, and Joseph.
CCC, 533, 1655

Q: How did Jesus share God's love with all people?

A: Jesus went from town to town teaching people about God. He treated all people with respect. He shared the news of God's love with everyone.
CCC, 544, 561

Q: What are commandments?

A: Commandments are laws given to us by God.
CCC, 2056–2058

Q: How do we follow the Great Commandment that Jesus gave us?

A: We follow the Great Commandment when we love God, ourselves, and others. *CCC, 2055*

Q: What do we do throughout the Church year?

A: All year long the Church gathers to thank God for his great love. Together, we praise God. We celebrate all that Jesus did for us.
CCC, 1168, 1171, 1172

Q: What do we celebrate during Ordinary Time?

A: During Ordinary Time we celebrate Jesus' life and teachings. *CCC, 1163, 1168, 1172, 1173, 1195*

Q: Who are the Apostles?

A: The Apostles were the twelve men Jesus chose to lead his followers. *CCC, 858*

Q: What prayer did Jesus teach his followers?

A: Jesus taught his followers the Lord's Prayer. We also call this prayer the Our Father. *CCC, 2759, 2761*

Q: What is Pentecost?

A: Pentecost is the day the Holy Spirit came to Jesus' followers. *CCC, 1076*

Q: What is the Church?

A: The Church is all the people who are baptized in Jesus and follow his teachings. *CCC, 752, 759*

Q: Who leads and cares for the Church?

A: The pope and bishops lead and care for the whole Church. *CCC, 861, 862, 869*

Q: What is Advent?

A: Advent is a special time when we get ready for the coming of God's Son, Jesus. *CCC, 524*

Q: What do we celebrate at Christmas?

A: At Christmas we celebrate the birth of the Son of God, Jesus. *CCC, 1171*

Q: What is a parish?

A: A parish is a group of Catholics who join together to share God's love. *CCC, 2179*

Q: What is a sacrament?

A: A sacrament is a special sign given to us by Jesus that gives us his love. *CCC, 1131*

Q: What is Baptism?

A: Baptism is the sacrament in which we become children of God and members of the Church. *CCC, 1213*

Q: What is grace?

A: Grace is God's life in us. *CCC, 1997*

Q: What happens when we celebrate the Sacrament of Penance and Reconciliation?

A: When we celebrate the Sacrament of Penance and Reconciliation, we receive and celebrate God's forgiveness. *CCC, 1422, 1440*

Q: What is Lent?

A: Lent is a special time to get ready for the Church's celebration of Jesus' Resurrection. *CCC, 1438*

Q: What is the Eucharist?

A: The Eucharist is the sacrament in which, by the power of the Holy Spirit, the bread and wine become the Body and Blood of Jesus Christ. *CCC, 1323, 1413*

Q: What is the Mass?

A: The Mass is the celebration of the Eucharist. *CCC, 1382*

Q: What do we do at Mass?

A: At Mass we gather to worship God. We listen to God's Word. Our gifts of bread and wine become the Body and Blood of Christ, which are received in Holy Communion. *CCC, 1346, 1348, 1355*

Q: **What is the Gospel?**

A: The Gospel is the Good News about Jesus Christ and his teachings. *CCC*, 125

Q: **Why do we honor Mary and the saints?**

A: The Church honors Mary because she is the Mother of Jesus, God the Son. The Church honors the saints because they are followers of Jesus who have died and now live forever with God. *CCC*, 828, 829, 2683

Q: **How can we care for the gifts of God's creation?**

A: God wants us to use our gifts and talents to care for all people. He also wants us to care for all creation. *CCC*, 299, 2415

Q: **What do we celebrate during Easter?**

A: During Easter we celebrate that Jesus Christ rose from the dead. *CCC*, 1169

Resources
for the Family

I n this section, you will find a treasury of resources to help build up your Catholic Identity at home, in your parish, and in the community. Learn more about key Catholic teachings from the themes of your child's *Celebrating Catholic Identity* retreats: **CREED, LITURGY & SACRAMENTS, MORALITY,** and **PRAYER**. For each theme, you will find Catholic prayers, practices, and devotions to share with those you love—and make a part of your daily lives as a Catholic family!

Family: "the place where parents pass on the faith to their children."

—Pope Francis
Apostolic Exhortation *Evangelii Gaudium*, 66

Spirituality and Your First-Grade Child

Your first grader is open, curious, spontaneous, and full of energy. Children at this age move easily between the worlds of reality and imagination. This gives them a natural foundation for a lifelong response to the joys and mysteries of God. Find opportunities to allow your child to use the arts to express the faith. You can draw pictures together, make up stories, sing songs, and act out simple plays in order to bring the lessons of faith alive for your child. Your child is highly imaginative but has a limited attention span. You may find it helpful to vary activities by moving from quiet work to physical movement. Be sure to allow time for silence and prayer together.

First graders are developing concrete thinking skills. They learn quickly by active involvement with concrete things and experiences. For example, talk to your child about the senses we use as we gather to worship, such as *seeing* the altar, *blessing* ourselves with holy water, and *smelling* incense and candles. Encourage participation in tactile experiences of faith and discuss what our participation means.

Your first grader is growing in the ability to work cooperatively with others. When engaging your child in family activities, stress the importance of love and mutual respect toward family members and others.*

*See *Catechetical Formation in Chaste Living*, United States Conference of Catholic Bishops, #1

Jesus Christ, the Son of God

Jesus is God the Son who became one of us. He grew up in a family. Jesus prayed every morning and every night with his mother, Mary, and his foster father, Joseph. Jesus' family showed their love for God and one another.

In the Nicene Creed, we express our belief in Jesus. Explain to your child that the Nicene Creed is the creed we often pray at Mass on Sunday. Pray the Creed together and note the parts that refer to Jesus.

Nicene Creed

I believe in one God,
　　the Father almighty,
　　maker of heaven and earth,
　　of all things visible and invisible.

I believe in one Lord Jesus Christ,
　　the Only Begotten Son of God,
　　born of the Father before all ages.
　　God from God, Light from Light,
　　true God from true God,
　　begotten, not made, consubstantial
　　　　with the Father;
　　through him all things were made.
　　For us men and for our salvation
　　　　he came down from heaven,
　　and by the Holy Spirit
　　　　was incarnate of the Virgin Mary,
　　　　and became man.

For our sake he was crucified
　　　　under Pontius Pilate,
　　he suffered death and was buried,
　　and rose again on the third day
　　　　in accordance with the Scriptures.
　　He ascended into heaven
　　　　and is seated at the right hand
　　　　of the Father.
　　He will come again in glory to judge
　　　　the living and the dead
　　　　and his kingdom will have no end.

I believe in the Holy Spirit, the Lord,
　　the giver of life,
　　who proceeds from the Father and the Son,
　　who with the Father and the Son is
　　　　adored and glorified,
　　who has spoken through the prophets.

I believe in one, holy, catholic
　　and apostolic Church.
I confess one Baptism for the
　　forgiveness of sins
and I look forward to the resurrection of the
　　dead and the life of the world to come.
Amen.

345

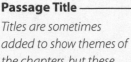
Book

Chapter

Verse

Passage

119   Luke, |10|

Passage Title

Titles are sometimes added to show themes of the chapters, but these titles are not part of the actual words of the Bible.

Praise of the Father |21| *t u**At that very moment he rejoiced [in] the holy Spirit and said, "I give you praise, Father, Lord of heaven and earth, for although you have hidden these things from the wise and the learned you have revealed them to the childlike. Yes, Father, such has been your gracious will. 22 *v*All things have been handed over to me by my Father. No one knows who the Son is except the Father, and who the Father is except the Son and anyone to whom the Son wishes to reveal him."

A passage is a section of a chapter made up of a number of verses.

This passage shows Luke 10:21–22, which means: the Gospel of Luke, chapter ten, verses twenty-one to twenty-two.

Reading the Bible . . . in Five Easy Steps

When you are given a Scripture passage to read, here are five easy steps that will help you to find it! With your child, follow these steps to look up **Lk 10:21–22**.

1. **Find the book.** When the name of the book is abbreviated, locate the meaning of the abbreviation on the contents pages at the beginning of your Bible. *Lk* stands for Luke, one of the four Gospels.

2. **Find the page.** Your Bible's contents pages will also show the page on which the book begins. Turn to that page within your Bible.

3. **Find the chapter.** Once you arrive at the page where the book begins, keep turning the pages forward until you find the right chapter. The image above shows you how a chapter number is usually displayed on a typical Bible page. You are looking for chapter **10** in Luke.

4. **Find the verses.** Once you find the right chapter, locate the verse or verses you need within the chapter. The image above also shows you how verse numbers will look on a typical Bible page. You are looking for verses **21** and **22**.

5. **Start reading!**

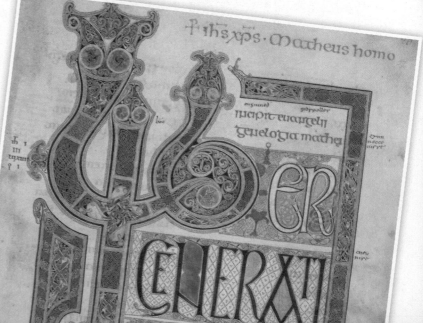

The Power of Grace

How do we live as disciples of Jesus? Through the power of God's grace, we can grow in our friendship with God. Grace is a share in God's life and love. We receive grace at our Baptism and when we receive the other sacraments. The water of Baptism is a sign of the life that God gives us through his grace. Throughout our lives, grace helps us respond to God with love. It gives us the strength to live as Jesus' disciples.

A Virtuous Life

A virtue is a good habit that helps us to act according to God's plan for us. Virtues help guide our conduct with the help of God's grace. The virtues of faith, hope, and charity are theological virtues. These virtues are called theological virtues because they are gifts from God.

An Act of Faith

O God, we believe in all that Jesus has
    taught us about you.
We place all our trust in you
    because of your great love for us.

An Act of Hope

O God, we never give up on your love.
We have hope and will work for your
kingdom to come and for a life that
lasts forever with you in heaven.

An Act of Love

O God, we love you above all things.
Help us to love ourselves and one another
as Jesus taught us to do.

Holy Days of Obligation

The liturgy is the official public prayer of the Church. In the liturgy we gather as a community joined to Christ to celebrate what we believe. The Church year is based on the life of Christ and the celebration of his life in the liturgy. The Church's year is called the liturgical year. In one liturgical year we recall and celebrate the whole life of Jesus Christ. We also honor Mary and the saints, who show us how to live as disciples of Jesus.

Each Sunday of the liturgical year is a great celebration of the Church, or a solemnity. In addition to each Sunday, there are other solemnities in the liturgical year on which we are obliged to attend Mass to give special honor to Jesus Christ for the salvation he has given to us. These are called holy days of obligation.

Holy days of obligation celebrated by the Church in the United States:

- **Solemnity of Mary, Mother of God (January 1)**
- **Ascension (when celebrated on Thursday during the Easter season*)**
- **Assumption of Mary (August 15)**
- **All Saints' Day (November 1)**
- **Immaculate Conception (December 8)**
- **Christmas (December 25)**

Some dioceses celebrate the Ascension on the following Sunday.

A Roadmap to Happiness

What makes your family happy? When we live as Jesus' disciples, we can find true happiness. The Beatitudes are Jesus' teachings that describe the way to live as his disciples. In the Beatitudes the word *blessed* means "happy."

The Beatitudes	What the Beatitudes Mean for Us
"Blessed are the poor in spirit, for theirs is the kingdom of heaven."	We are "poor in spirit" when we depend on God and make God more important than anyone or anything else in our lives.
"Blessed are they who mourn, for they will be comforted."	We "mourn" when we are sad because of the selfish ways people treat each other.
"Blessed are the meek, for they will inherit the land."	We are "meek" when we are patient, kind, and respectful to all people, even those who do not respect us.
"Blessed are they who hunger and thirst for righteousness, for they will be satisfied."	We "hunger and thirst for righteousness" when we search for justice and treat everyone fairly.
"Blessed are the merciful, for they will be shown mercy."	We are "merciful" when we forgive others and do not take revenge on those who hurt us.
"Blessed are the clean of heart, for they will see God."	We are "clean of heart" when we are faithful to God's teachings and try to see God in all people and all situations.
"Blessed are the peacemakers, for they will be called children of God."	We are "peacemakers" when we treat others with love and respect and when we help others to stop fighting and make peace.
"Blessed are they who are persecuted for the sake of righteousness, for theirs is the kingdom of heaven." Matthew 5:3–10	We are "persecuted for the sake of righteousness" when others disrespect us for living as disciples of Jesus and following his example.

Following Jesus

Jesus gave us two commandments that help us to follow the way he lived. Read and talk about these commandments as a family. Let them guide all your relationships—at home, at school, in the parish, and in the community.

Great Commandment

"You shall love the Lord, your God, with all your heart, with all your soul, and with all your mind. This is the greatest and the first commandment. The second is like it: You shall love your neighbor as yourself." (Matthew 22:37–39)

New Commandment

"I give you a new commandment: love one another. As I have loved you, so you also should love one another. This is how all will know that you are my disciples, if you have love for one another." (John 13:34–35)

Peace and Justice

As disciples of Jesus, we must commit to justice and become peacemakers in every context of our lives. Justice is based on the simple fact that all people have human dignity, the value and worth that we share because God created us in his image and likeness. In Scripture, we find that God's peace, which is more than just the absence of war and violence, is realized when everyone lives in true harmony with one another and with God's creation.

"Justice will bring about peace; right will produce calm and security."

(Isaiah 32:17)

Prayer of Saint Francis of Assisi

This prayer for peace is attributed to Saint Francis of Assisi.

Lord, make me an instrument of your peace:
where there is hatred, let me sow love;
where there is injury, pardon;
where there is doubt, faith;
where there is despair, hope;
where there is darkness, light;
where there is sadness, joy.

O Divine Master, grant that I may not so much seek
to be consoled as to console,
to be understood as to understand,
to be loved as to love.

For it is in giving that we receive,
it is in pardoning that we are pardoned,
it is in dying that we are born to eternal life.
Amen.

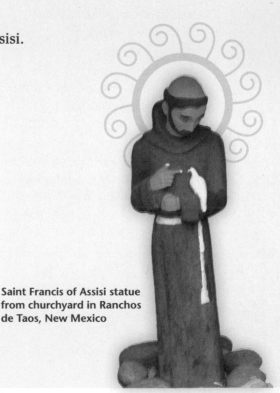

Saint Francis of Assisi statue from churchyard in Ranchos de Taos, New Mexico

Praying the Rosary

The Rosary is among traditional expressions of prayer we call devotions. The Mysteries of the Rosary are taken from the lives of Jesus and Mary. Reflecting on each Mystery as we pray the Rosary helps to draw us into the mystery of Jesus Christ among us.

The Virgin Mary, Ghent Altarpiece, Saint Bavo Cathedral, Ghent, Belgium, by Jan van Eyck (1429)

Mysteries of the Rosary

Joyful Mysteries
The Annunciation
The Visitation
The Birth of Jesus
The Presentation of Jesus in the Temple
The Finding of the Child Jesus in the Temple

Sorrowful Mysteries
The Agony in the Garden
The Scourging at the Pillar
The Crowning with Thorns
The Carrying of the Cross
The Crucifixion and Death of Jesus

Glorious Mysteries
The Resurrection
The Ascension
The Descent of the Holy Spirit upon the
    Apostles
The Assumption of Mary into Heaven
The Coronation of Mary as Queen of Heaven

The Mysteries of Light
Jesus' Baptism in the Jordan
The Miracle at the Wedding at Cana
Jesus Announces the Kingdom of God
The Transfiguration
The Institution of the Eucharist

The Rosary

Praying the Rosary creates a peaceful rhythm of prayer during which we can reflect on the Mysteries of the Rosary, special times in the lives of Jesus and Mary. Follow the numbered steps to pray the Rosary.

5 Pray a Glory Be to the Father after each set of small beads.

End

6 Pray the Hail, Holy Queen to end the rosary.

4 Pray a Hail Mary at every small bead.

3 Pray an Our Father at every large bead.

2 Then pray the Apostles' Creed.

1 Start with the Sign of the Cross.

Start

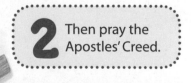